AROUND SCOTLAND IN

8 0

TREASURES

A Unique Guide to an Alternative and
Amazing Scotland **by David Keith**

Around Scotland in 80 Treasures

David Keith

There's gold in them hills I tell thee!

Whilst this is actually a statement of fact for some of the hills and mountains of Scotland, it's not the precious metal we will be searching for in this book. Nor is it the legendary and still undiscovered Jacobite treasure from 1745. The type of treasure that we are seeking in this book is one that is far more valuable...memories! How can you put a value on treasured memories? You can't really because it is something that is entirely personal to you as an individual, but it does beg the question...

What is treasure?

The Oxford English Dictionary states: Treasure – noun – a quantity of precious metals, gems, or other valuable objects.

Okay fair enough that's the literal meaning, but it leads to a second question...

Does treasure *always* have to be an object that we can hold in our hands?

The simple answer is no.

This brings us onto a third question...

If treasure isn't always something that we cradle in our hands, can it be something we see and behold?

Of course it can. It is our ability to observe and enjoy beautiful sights, sounds and sensations that give us treasured moments; events that add depth and value to our lives, enabling us to build lifelong memories.

Let's be honest, true treasure is never easily found without at least a bit of effort, although some are lucky enough to just stumble upon it. This book is intended to be an enabler; allow yourself to be lured away from the well-worn track, blasted along by so many who are completely oblivious to what lies just beyond. Give yourself the opportunity to explore - only then will you be properly rewarded. If you find yourself motivated to get out and explore the locations listed (which I hope you do), be aware that some do require a lot more effort and preparation to get to than others, but rest assured they will all pique your interest in some way. Hopefully you'll find yourself saying things like "that was amazing!" or "that was well worth the effort" or even just "that was nice". Whatever your reaction I truly hope that you enjoy the searching and the discovering as much as I have.

Why Scotland?

Being born and raised in Scotland is a good starting point, but that is only the beginning. Both my wife Helen and I are very fortunate to have travelled extensively around Scotland during our careers as tour guides, which we both loved but a life on the road doesn't last forever. By combining our knowledge and experience coupled with a shared passion for interesting and special places, Around Scotland in 80 Treasures was a natural evolution. Although we are no longer constantly on the road we haven't stopped searching because there are always new places to find and explore, especially in Scotland.

Scotland has so much to offer in the way of unique and amazing experiences in less well known places, and just because Scotland may not have the highest mountains, the longest beaches, the widest rivers in the world, that doesn't matter because it is simply one of the most amazing places to explore - and don't just take our word for it, Scotland was voted the most beautiful country in the world by Rough Guide readers in 2017. There is just something very special about the place; it somehow gets under your skin and once you've had a taste you just end up wanting more.

What is it that creates that something special? The answer is the combination of:

- the landscapes that you find in Scotland and
- the people coupled with their history, passion and humour who have made this place home over many millennia

It is this variety that appeals to so many and draws people from across the globe to visit and seek out *their* Scotland. This book has been written to enhance that very unique and personal experience as well as make you smile whilst reading it.

Brief background to Scotland

Geology

Scotland's geological journey has been incredibly long, varied and at times momentous. In the dim and distant past it has been a shallow tropical sea, a desert, a jungle, seriously mountainous (as in Himalayas serious) and spotted with great (and small) volcanoes. After all this activity, the landscapes that were left behind were covered and worn down by sheets of glacial ice to eventually give us what we have today. Indeed it is this distant past that gives Scotland its wealth of different rock types, which in turn provides the diversity of landscapes that has helped form the special places that we can freely enjoy today, and that feature in this book.

Land

Scotland comprises of 30,414 square miles (78,770 square kilometres) of land. To give some context it is about the size of Panama in Central America or the Czech Republic in Central Europe. Scotland has over 10,000 miles of coastline (including its many hundreds of islands) and over 31,000 freshwater lochs (lakes) and lochans (small lakes).

Emblems

Scotland has the unicorn as its national animal, a mythological creature that exists only in our imaginations - thankfully there are no rules regarding whether a creature actually has to exist for it to be adopted as your national animal! It has the thistle, a tough prickly yet beautiful purple flowering plant, as its national emblem. The harebell (which is also known as the Scottish bluebell) is its national flower...that flowery fact may come as a surprise to some people because many think that the thistle *is* the flower of Scotland! There are two flags that are unique to Scotland; one is the national flag (the Saltire), which is a white X-shaped cross on a light blue background, and the other is the Royal flag (the Lion Rampant) which consists of a red lion on a gold background.

People

Often when you read about the history of Scotland's people words like 'turbulent' and 'violent' are used! There is truth in this of course and some of the treasures referred to in this book reflect that turbulence, however it could also be said that Scotland's history is nothing more than a reflection of human history in general. To take such a narrow view in focussing on battles and conflict does a great disservice to all the amazing writers, inventors, engineers, pioneers, scientists, architects, religious figures, sports people and politicians, who through their work have helped create the modern world that we live in today. The next time you go to an Automated Teller Machine (ATM) and use your Personal Identification Number (PIN) just remember it was a Scotsman by the name of James Goodfellow from Paisley who invented that very useful technology! Tough times may help form character, but they certainly do not make a person or a nation.

Scotland's population is currently between 5.3 and 5.4 million people, the highest it has ever been, however there are many more millions of people worldwide who are either directly Scots-born or are from Scots descent. My own family are part of this very broad diaspora, with one brother and his family in Australia and a cousin and her family in Singapore.

About 80 Treasures

The eighty treasures in this book have been specially selected to take you on a wide ranging journey that will hopefully spark new and inspiring thoughts, make you smile, and may even be life enhancing.

The Treasures are listed under the following categories:

- Ecclesiastical and Spiritual
- Castles and Fortifications
- Beauty Spots
- Food and Drink
- Walks
- Sites of Historic Interest and Intrigue

Each treasure has a description coupled with some history (if appropriate) and photograph(s) to add some context and to convey why the place is special. There is a simple map at the beginning of each section to act as a rough guide on the location of each treasure (should you wish to go exploring for yourself). There are some basic directions to help you find the treasures although I'd recommend doing a little bit more research on certain locations to help with navigation before setting off on your own adventures.

I hope that you enjoy this book and that it helps you discover a different and much more fascinating Scotland than the one often described in many standard books.

Happy travels – Safe Oot Safe In, as we say in the Scottish Borders.

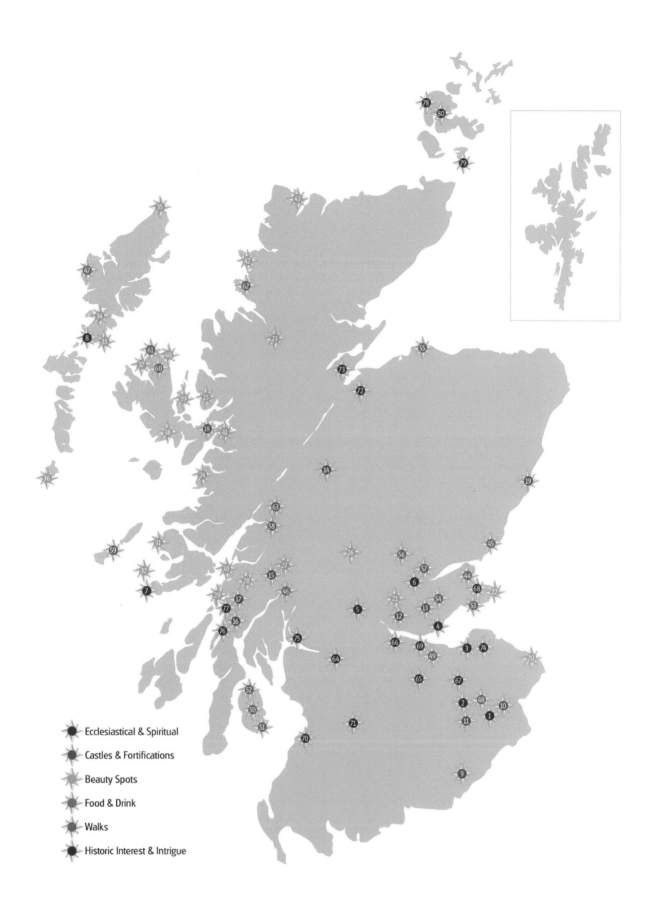

Ecclesiastical & Spiritual

Castles & Fortifications

Beauty Spots

Food & Drink

Walks

Historic Interest & Intrigue

List of Treasures:

Ecclesiastical and Spiritual

1. **Dryburgh Abbey**
2. **Stow Holy Well**
3. **Seton Collegiate Church**
4. **Inchcolm Abbey**
5. **Inchmahome Priory**
6. **Dupplin Pictish Cross**
7. **Isle of Iona**
8. **St Clement's Church**

Castles and Fortifications

9. **Hermitage Castle**
10. **Old Roxburgh Castle**
11. **Fatlips Castle**
12. **Dollar Glen/Castle Campbell**
13. **Loch Leven Castle**
14. **Dun Da-Lamh Pictish Fort**
15. **Kilchurn Castle**
16. **Dunadd Hill Fort**
17. **Carnasserie Castle**
18. **Castle Moil**
19. **Dunnottar Castle**

Beauty Spots

20. **St Abbs Head and Coldingham Bay**
21. **Rumbling Brig (bridge)**
22. **Wormistoune House & Gardens**
23. **Corrieshalloch Gorge**
24. **Loch Morar and silver sands**
25. **Bealach Na Ba**
26. **Fortingall Yew Tree**
27. **Glen Orchy Falls**
28. **Glen Lonan (Road of the Kings)**
29. **Easdale (Isle of Seil) and Isle of Easdale**
30. **Isle of Kerrera**
31. **Calgary Bay**
32. **Isle of Staffa**
33. **The Golden Road**
34. **Luskentyre and Hushinish beaches**
35. **The Butt of Lewis**
36. **Isles of Barra and Vatersay**
37. **Faerie Glen**
38. **Loch Coruisk boat trip**
39. **Isle of Raasay**
40. **Loch Shianta**

41. Kylerhea - Glenelg Ferry and Brochs
42. Achmelvich beach and Lochinver Larder
43. Smoo Cave

Food and Drink

44. Cromars Fish and Chip Shop
45. Arbroath Smokies and Forfar Bridies
46. Loch Fyne Oyster Bar and Fyne Ales
47. Abhainn Dearg Distillery

Walks

48. Eildon Hills and Trimontium
49. Roslin Glen & Castle
50. Goat Fell
51. Glenashdale
52. North Glen Sannox Pools and Falls
53. Elie Chain Walk
54. The Lomond Hills (Paps of Fife)
55. Primrose Bay
56. Birks of Aberfeldy
57. Birnam Oak and Birnam Hill
58. The Lost Valley
59. The Ringing Stone
60. The Table, Quiraing
61. Rubha Hunish
62. Stac Pollaidh
63. Steall Falls and the Nevis Gorge

Sites of Historic Interest and Intrigue

64. The Govan Stones
65. The Great Polish Map of Scotland
66. The Kelpies
67. Soutra Aisle
68. Dunino Den
69. Gilmerton Cove
70. The Robert Burns Birthplace Museum
71. St Bride's Kirk
72. Culloden Battlefield
73. The Clootie Well
74. Traprain Law
75. Hill House
76. Arichonan Township
77. Kilmartin and Kilmartin Glen
78. Skara Brae
79. Tomb of the Eagles
80. Ness and Ring of Brodgar

Ecclesiastical and Spiritual

Scotland has had its fair share of religious 'ups and downs' over the years and this is reflected in many of the treasures in this section. Whether atheist, agnostic or spiritual it is hard not to appreciate at least some of the buildings and monuments that Christianity has inspired in Scotland.

1. Dryburgh Abbey

What you'll discover:

I have to admit to a certain bias here because on the eighth of October 2016 Helen and I tied the knot (quite literally) and got married in the gorgeous ruins of Dryburgh Abbey. We enjoyed a Humanist ceremony, during which we conducted an old Scottish tradition of symbolically tying two pieces of material (we chose ribbons in our own tartans) together around our hands, thus demonstrating the joining together of two individuals as one or simply 'tying the knot'. We were blessed with the most amazing day bathed in sunshine (there had been some concern as we were having an outdoor ceremony in autumn in Scotland, but thankfully for us fortune favours the brave!) and our special day became a tiny part of the Abbey's long history.

The Abbey was the last of the four great Border Abbeys to be built established in 1150 CE by the Premonstratensian order, and it would have been a splendid collection of buildings in its time. However like each of the Border Abbeys including Melrose, Kelso and Jedburgh, it fell foul of war with the English and was subsequently abandoned after the Reformation in 1560 CE. The ruins visible today are set within beautiful parkland grounds with great towering mature trees, one of which is an ancient Yew tree dating back to at least the foundation of the Abbey if not before. Coupled with the steady calming flow of the River Tweed which meanders nearby, Dryburgh Abbey has an incredibly tranquil feel about it. Once in the grounds, as well as getting a feel for monastic life you can visit the graves of the famous writer Sir Walter Scott, and nearby the Commander in Chief of the British Expeditionary Force (BEF) during the First World War, Field Marshal Douglas Haig.

After you have visited the Abbey it is worth taking a short walk down to the River Tweed to the Temple of the Muses, which is a lovely, quiet and peaceful place. Locally there are other great points of interest which could also be viewed as wee treasures of their own such as the Wallace Statue and Scott's View. The statue was the first in the world to be erected to celebrate William Wallace, and although impressive it does make this famous Scottish hero look a bit like a Greek God. This was due to a mild obsession with Greek mythology by the statue's financier and original owner David Steuart Erskine (the eleventh Earl of Buchan), but don't let that minor point stop you from going to see it. Scott's View is just over a mile away from the Wallace Statue and is definitely worth stopping to admire.

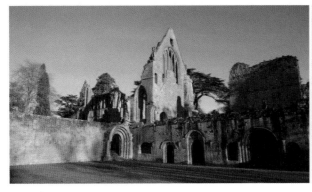

How to get there:

Dryburgh Abbey is near the village of St Boswells. Drive east out of St Boswells on the road to Kelso (the B6404) and once you have crossed the River Tweed at the Mertoun Bridge, take a left onto the B6356 and simply follow the road until you come to the Abbey car park. If travelling from the north, continue past the viewpoint at Scott's View and the Wallace Statue car park, and thereafter follow the brown information signs for the Abbey. Dryburgh is under the ownership of Historic Environment Scotland and has an admission charge.

2. Stow Holy Well

What you'll discover:

Having moved to Stow in the Scottish Borders in 2013 (one the best things Helen and I have ever done except getting married and rescuing our dog Tig), we began to explore our new home and discovered there was an ancient Holy Well just south of the village. Stow Holy Well is also known as Our Lady's Well and is one of the most ancient Christian sites in southern Scotland, dating back to the late Roman period. Many early Christian sites often adopted what were already important pre-Christian sites - in all likelihood the natural spring that feeds the well would have been known about and revered by many local people long before Christianity arrived in this area of Scotland. The well is tucked away just below the A7 road, in what some may view as an unlikely place to find treasure, but not so because once you are there the fast-paced world becomes a distant distraction. I have to admit though that a bit of imagination is required to try and envisage what it would have been like when it was a shrine to the Virgin Mary.

The name of the village of Stow derives from Germanic Anglo-Saxon meaning "holy place" and it is of no surprise that the ruin of an old church and very impressive more modern church still stand in the village today. When you get to the well it is nice to just take a moment to sit next to the water. You'll begin to forget that there is a main road literally about twenty metres away as you watch the natural spring water bubbling up through the sediment in the base of the well. It is this ability to transport you into a world of seclusion that makes this place so special. Is the water drinkable? I have sampled it on numerous occasions and have had no ill effects; in fact it tastes wonderful so why not give it a go? If you are interested in finding out more about the local history there is an interesting archive located in the village hall which currently opens three days a week.

How to get there:

It is best to park in the village of Stow and walk to the old humped bridge, referred to locally as the subscription bridge, which was built to help the local population get to church. Climb the stile over the fence in the direction of Galashiels where there is a simple way marker pointing to 'Our Lady's Well' and walk along the bank of the Gala Water through a coppice of scrubby hawthorn bushes (take adequate footwear as it can be muddy). Cross the field following the general direction of the burn (stream), you'll pass on the left what was the old outdoor curling rink and as you cross another fence veer to the left towards the road and you will see an enclosed area ahead of you. You've made it. Keep dogs on a lead if there is livestock in the fields.

3. Seton Collegiate Church

What you'll discover:

In the fifteenth century it wasn't unusual for wealthy nobility in the local area around Edinburgh and further afield to build family chapels as an expression of their devotion to the Catholic Church, as well as to show off some of their own wealth and status. Within these private churches the family would employ the services of a college of canons or priests to pray for their family's souls and salvation. This gathering together of canons/priests into a college or community is where the word 'collegiate' comes from. It is within this historical context that Seton Collegiate Church has its origins.

Seton started life in the 1470s when the local Seton family decided to build a church as their private chapel. It is a fine place which has a nice calming feel about it, a kind of serenity that is hard to find these days. This is largely due to the church's location off the main tourist trail so it is very rarely (if ever) overrun by visitors - when you visit there is ample opportunity to just quietly wander around enjoying the architecture, history and peace that is on offer. Of course it has seen its fair share of troubles, especially during the 'Rough Wooing' (which is briefly explained in treasure number 5) in the 1540s which lead to damage and theft by English soldiers, to then be quickly followed by the Reformation of the Church in Scotland in 1560 when Scotland became officially Calvinist. This religious change away from Catholicism effectively ended collegiate life at Seton, although the church continued to function in a reduced form. During the Jacobite uprisings of 1715 and 1745, the structure was damaged again particularly in the aftermath of the nearby Battle of Prestonpans on the twenty-first of September 1745 which resulted in a swift and very decisive victory for the Jacobites. For those interested in finding out more about the battle, there is a viewpoint nearby on the edge of the town of Prestonpans which has information boards describing the event.

Despite the damage inflicted to the church, it does have some fine and very interesting features, a fascinating history, lovely well kept grounds with medicinal herbs, and above all no maddening crowds which helps those who are looking to get away from it all and enjoy a bit of peace and quiet.

How to get there:

Exit the A1 road at Tranent and initially follow signs for Prestonpans, then follow signs to Longniddry on the A198. Once you are on the A198 keep your wits about you because the entrance to the Church car park is upon you before you know it. Once parked simply follow the path through the woods to the entrance to the Church. The Church is under the ownership of Historic Environment Scotland, is open seasonally (April - October), and has an admission charge.

4. Inchcolm Abbey

What you'll discover:

In early Christianity there was a desire by monks to seek out isolation and seclusion - quite often these early Christians would end up in some pretty harsh uninhabited places, living off the most meagre of rations and having no unnecessary personal belongings or luxuries. Theirs was a simple life devoid of distractions where they would devote themselves to prayer and being closer to God. Being away from it all and choosing isolation is the key reason why you find so many ancient Christian buildings right across the world that are located in what would appear through modern eyes as being obscure and impractical places.

Inchcolm, meaning Columba's Isle (although there is no record of St Columba having ever been there), is sometimes referred to as the 'Iona of the East' (Iona is featured in treasure number 7). It fits right into the 'isolation' way of thinking as it is located on a small rocky island (inch) out in the deep waters of the Firth (estuary) of Forth. The original idea to build a monastery came from King Alexander I of Scotland after he was shipwrecked and found refuge in what he called a 'hermit's hovel' on the island. The hermit provided food - consisting of milk from his cow, and oysters - and shelter to the King. Although Alexander died before construction of the monastery began, his brother, David I, established an island priory which later became Inchcolm Abbey.

Although the Abbey's ruins are the best preserved of any monastic building in Scotland, they still suffered from English aggression during the Scottish Wars of Independence in the fourteenth century. You can also see more recent additions in the form of gun batteries, the earliest having been built in 1795 during the Napoleonic Wars. During the World Wars of the twentieth century, Inchcolm was again heavily fortified. When visiting Helen and I experienced a different type of aerial assault - it was of an avian kind from some very protective nesting gulls. The guide we met referred to this period on the island as 'Gullmagedon' - he wasn't wrong!

As you explore the ruins, don't miss the very rare example of a thirteenth century painted scene, the Latin inscription in the warming room, and the Viking hogback stone located in the island's museum (you can read more about hogback stones in treasure number 64).

It is not just the Abbey and the island with its bird life and seals that are a draw but also the journey to get there and back. From the ferry you get amazing views of the three very impressive bridges that span the River Forth. The crossing point between North and South Queensferry is the only place in the world where you can see three functioning bridges that were designed and built in three separate centuries - the Forth (Rail) Bridge in 1890, the Forth Road Bridge in 1964, and the Queensferry Crossing in 2017.

How to get there:

Take a boat trip from the pier at South Queensferry located just off the A90. The Abbey is under the ownership of Historic Environment Scotland, is open seasonally (April - October) and has an admission charge. Check before you travel as the boats may be disrupted by weather. Please note the boat trip and abbey admission are charged separately.

5. Inchmahome Priory

What you'll discover:

If you were ever looking for a sheltered inland island paradise in Scotland to establish a monastic settlement, Inchmahome would have to be near the top of your list due to its seclusion, tranquillity and the opportunity of self-sufficiency. The name 'Inchmahome' is a corruption of the Gaelic 'Innis (meaning island) MoCholmaig'. It is a low lying, fertile, wooded island and the largest of three found in the Lake of Menteith. You may be wondering why it is not called the Loch of Menteith - this is due to the loch being renamed a lake in the early 1800s during a successful advertising campaign to make the place sound more appealing to tourists from England who were travelling to the area by rail. Many of these visitors would have also been inspired to visit the area after reading popular literature of the time such as 'The Lady of the Lake' and 'Rob Roy' written by Sir Walter Scott.

On my first visit to Inchmahome, the ten minute journey across the Lake of Menteith was memorable - it was a calm but very misty morning where I couldn't even see the island. The ferryman was an entertaining chap; he reassured me and my fellow passengers that we had nothing to worry about because he could do the journey with his eyes shut. Once on the island the mist did begin to lift and I explored the priory ruins. Most of the ruins that you can see today date from the time of the priory's construction, which started in 1238. It was established and built by the Augustinian order, and although it was tucked away it was visited on no less than three occasions by King Robert the Bruce in the early 1300s, apparently for solitude and sanctuary, but more likely he intended to have some choice 'diplomatic' words with the Prior who supported Edward I of England.

During a period known as the 'rough wooing', which began in the early 1540s, Henry VIII of England constantly invaded Scotland to put pressure on the Scots to acquiesce to his demands that the Treaty of Greenwich be upheld - the agreement being that Mary Queen of Scots would marry Henry's son Edward. In 1547, Mary was brought to Inchmahome by her mother to protect her from the invading army. Although Henry was dead by this time, his loyal friend Lord Somerset continued to press on with Henry's intention of forcing the marriage. Thankfully she was safe at Inchmahome and not long after this she was sent to live in France under the protection of the French royal court.

Whilst on the island it's worth going for a wander through the trees, some of which are believed to be five hundred years old. Inchmahome Priory is a special place with a special vibe.

How to get there:

Take the boat to Inchmahome from the Port of Menteith, which is situated on the eastern side of the lake. Travel along the A81 or the A811 and then turn onto the B8034. The island and Priory are under the ownership of Historic Environment Scotland, open seasonally (April - October), and there is an admission charge.

6. Dupplin Pictish Cross

What you'll discover:

The Dupplin Cross is unique; there is nothing else like it in the world and it is absolutely fascinating, with more being understood about it all the time. It is referred to as being Pictish, and dates from the earlier part of the ninth century - a period in Scottish history that is still not fully understood by historians even today. A bit of background may be helpful here to explain who the Picts were because they (as a people) have been greatly misunderstood for many years. Much of the misunderstanding that surrounds the Picts has come from the fact that very little (virtually nothing) of what was or may have been written by the Picts has survived, making it very difficult for historians to get a real insight into who they were and how they saw themselves. The key artifacts that historians use to try and understand the Picts is their ornate and intriguing stone carvings, although even today there is confusion and much debate over what some of the Pictish symbols mean or represent. My own personal opinion is that some of the more obscure symbols such as the double disk with 'Z rod' could be from Druidic traditions, where the symbols may have represented abbreviations of names of certain skilled groups or crafts like temple builders, healers or seers.

So what do we know so far? Genetic science suggests that the Picts were the direct descendants of the first settlers who ventured north at the end of the last Ice Age. Their name comes from the Latin 'Picti' (first written in 297 CE) meaning 'painted ones'; they are also referred to as 'Pechts' in Old Norse and in the Scots tongue. In Old Welsh they were called the 'Pritani' or sometimes the 'Prethen' which then morphed into Brittanni and the word 'Briton'. Interestingly in the Old Welsh texts they are sometimes referred to as the 'old ones' - possibly due to the fact that the Picts retained old pre-Roman ways and customs. This is certainly possible given they lived north of both Hadrian's Wall and the Antonine Wall, meaning they were beyond direct Roman rule but not entirely away from Roman influence. This argument has been backed up by recent archaeological digs at a Pictish site near Rhynie in Aberdeenshire, where objects discovered include pottery fragments from Byzantine amphorae and glass from France dating to the late Roman period. With regards to the structure of Pictish society, sources point towards a well-organised Celtic society where their Kings or leaders wore beautifully ornate heavy necklaces called torques rather than crowns. They spoke a 'P-Celtic' language not dissimilar to Old Welsh or Brittonic (which still survives today in place names such as Aberfeldy, Dollar, Pitlochry and Cardenden, although their actual spoken language has gone).

The Dupplin Cross is covered in pictures and symbols, although unfortunately some of the finer detail has been eroded due to exposure to the Scottish weather over hundreds of years. Thankfully modern laser analysis of the stone has revealed more, including the name Constantine. Through extensive research it appears this refers to an early King Constantine of the Picts, who ruled during the late eighth/early ninth century. Using imagery and symbolism, the Picts carved the story of Constantine onto the Dupplin Cross, featuring references to their King preventing Viking raids, gaining control over the Scots of Dál Riata, and keeping the advances of the Northumbrians to the south at bay. It is only in more recent years with improved understanding that this particular story has come to light; previously many of the subtle meanings were missed by scholars or misinterpreted.

When visiting listen carefully to the guides because they are very knowledgeable, but at the same time open to alternative interpretations that you may have. They'll help you understand the carvings as well as the symbolism; you'll be amazed by what you learn. The Dupplin Cross is simply a fascinating piece of historic artwork!

How to get there:

The Dupplin Cross is located inside St Serfs Church in the village of Dunning, a short distance south of Perth. The most scenic way to get there is from Yetts o'Muckhart up Dunning Glen on the B934; however you can also travel from the main A9 road on either the B8062 or the B9141. The Church and Cross are owned by Historic Environment Scotland, open seasonally (April - October), and although there is no admission charge there is a suggested donation amount.

7. Isle of Iona

What you'll discover:

In the Dark Age before Christianity was brought to Iona by St Columba, there are references to the island being called 'Innis nan Druinich' meaning the 'Isle of the Druidic hermits' and 'Ì nam ban bòidheach' meaning the 'Isle of the beautiful woman'. These alternative names are interesting because, as previously mentioned, early Christianity adopted many pre-Christian sites which would have been used by the Druids previously - this would explain the reference to Druidic hermits. The Druids worshipped Mother Earth, so was the name the 'Isle of the beautiful woman' referring to the female in the form of Mother Earth? It is hard to say for sure but it is worth taking these older names into some consideration when writing about the history of the island. The more modern name Iona appears to mean 'Yew Place' which again is interesting as the Yew tree was important to pre-Christians (discussed more in treasure number 26) as it symbolised the cycle of life.

Today when the name Iona is mentioned there is an immediate association with St Columba, or 'Colum Cille' in his native tongue. Columba was an Irish warrior/abbot/monk and missionary. He was banished from Ireland after the Battle of Cul Dreimhne (the Battle of the Book) in 561 CE, which took place near what is today Drumcliff, County Sligo, over what can only be described in modern terms as 'a copyright issue'. Columba had made a copy of a new Psalter (book of psalms) without the permission of his superior St Finnian - who wasn't best pleased! Columba was set adrift upon the ocean currents to go wherever the Lord sent him. He landed at Iona (maybe because it was already a place of spiritual importance, or perhaps that's just where the currents happened to take him!), established a monastery, and from Iona he travelled to spread the Christian word around what became northern Scotland - he even had the first recorded sighting of the Loch Ness Monster in 565 CE.

Over time Iona became the hub of Christianity in Dark Age early Medieval Scotland. It was a renowned centre of learning with its influence reaching right across Scotland, Ireland, and into the North of England (although influence in the North of England waned after the Synod of Whitby in 664 CE). Iona became famous for its Abbey and in particular its Scriptorium, which produced the beautifully illustrated Iona Chronicle - thought to be the source for the early Irish Annuls and arguably the more famous Book of Kells, currently on display in Trinity College, Dublin. It is believed to have either been fully written or certainly started on Iona although it was moved to Kells in Ireland due to Viking raids on Iona in 794 CE.

Even though the original Abbey was abandoned in 849 CE it still remained a place of importance, proven by the fact that it is the final resting place of forty-eight ancient Kings of Scotland, as well as eight Norwegian and four Irish kings. Much of what you see today is a rebuild of the early thirteenth century

Benedictine Abbey. There are three Celtic Crosses (although there were three hundred and sixty originally) which scholars think may be the earliest examples of the cross and circle format so familiar to the Celtic Church.

Iona is one of those places that just calms you; as a place of solitude and sanctuary Iona certainly hits the spot perfectly. Whilst on Iona it is hard to feel hurried so take your time, visit the small craft shops and find a quiet spot. My favourite place is the White Strand of the Monks beach.

How to get there:

First you'll need to board the ferry from Oban to the Isle of Mull. From Craignure ferry terminal drive (or take the bus) to Fionnphort on the A849. Located at the end of the Ross of Mull, Fionnphort is where you board the small ferry to Iona. If time allows take a boat trip that includes the Isle of Staffa (treasure number 32).

8. St Clement's Church

What you'll discover:

St Clement's Church belonged to Clan MacLeod of Harris - the name MacLeod (or McLeod) translates into 'Son of the ugly one' or possibly 'Son of the ugly wolf'. I have a friend called Ewan McLeod whose physical appearance could well be described as a bit wolf-like - thankfully though in general their looks have improved over the years. Within clan society, the chief was the most important man; he was expected to be a strong leader, friend, arbiter, distributer of justice and the overall patriarch of his people (his 'clanna' - meaning children). For this to be done properly he had to have a good level of education and be knowledgeable about his own immediate world and its people but also the one beyond the boundaries of his ancestral lands. He commanded great respect and was to be fair in mind and action but yet fierce when the need arose. As well as being the main man in all matters clan-related there was also a spiritual side to their leadership. In fact quite a number of earlier (pre-Rodel Church) MacLeod chiefs were buried on the Isle of Iona indicating their strength of faith.

St Clement's Church - also known as Rodel Church - was commissioned by the eighth Clan Chief Alasdair, with construction starting in 1520. It is viewed as one of the best examples of pre-Reformation ecclesiastical architecture and is the only cruciform church to be found on the Western Isles of Scotland. He – along with two of his descendents – is buried inside the Church with Alasdair having arguably one of the finest wall tombs in Scotland. After the

Reformation of the Scottish Church in 1560, the church was abandoned as it was a Catholic place of worship and did not fit into the new reformist Calvinist model, so in all reality it wasn't used for very long as a place of worship although the cemetery continued to be used as a MacLeod burial site. As well as the history there are some fine views to be enjoyed.

How to get there:

St Clement's Church is located at the southern end of the A859, near Leverburgh. To get to the Isle of Harris you can choose from a number of different ferry options sailing into either Leverburgh from Berneray, or Tarbert from Uig on the Isle of Skye. The Church is in the care of Historic Environment Scotland and is free to visit.

Castles and Fortifications

Scotland has one of the highest concentrations of castles and fortifications in the world! Some of Scotland's castles have become visual icons of the country such as Edinburgh, Stirling and Eilean Donan. Go beyond the better known castles and forts you will find some amazing places to explore.

9. Hermitage Castle

What you'll discover:

In 2015 I worked as the steward at Hermitage Castle, located in an isolated, sparsely populated area of the Scottish Borders, a short distance from the border with England. During my time there the most common question I was asked was "why was the castle built *here*?" This question took a lot of explanation and background history to answer.

For the best part of three hundred years the Border country (north and south of the Scottish/English border) was a scene of almost perpetual violence and conflict. A culture and society developed from this adversity where fighting and bitter rivalries were the norm, and loyalty was to an individual or family first before any sense of nation - these people were called the Borders Reivers. For all intents and purposes they behaved and operated much like more modern mafia gangs, relying on theft, intimidation, violence and extortion to survive and at times thrive. There are words and sayings which exist in the English language today which find their origins in this tumultuous period. For example the origins of the word 'blackmail' relate to the payment of 'mail' - which was grain for rent - but the payment also covered protection of the payer's cattle - which were mostly black in colour - hence 'blackmail'. The word 'bereavement' is said to have its origins from when land/property/individuals were attacked by a band of Reivers - the loss of wealth/life meant the owner had been 'be-reived'.

Over the centuries there was one particular valley that earned the reputation of being the bloodiest - Liddesdale. It was due to the extreme levels of violence in Liddesdale and its close proximity to the border which gives us the answer to why Hermitage Castle was built where it was - to try and police what was a very dangerous area, and to defend the border in times of war. It is a dark, brooding and intimidating place, which was developed over three main stages during the fourteenth century and at each stage it became more menacing. What you see of the castle today is pretty much how it would have looked six hundred years ago. It was not built to be pretty.

On arrival there is a certain 'wow factor' because so much of the original castle is intact and it has a very imposing appearance. When inside the castle some people do get the shivers, particularly in the prison tower, but that may just be the wind… When visiting be sure to go to the chapel site and see the 'drowning pool' where it is said a giant Northumbrian lord called the 'Cout (count) of Kielder' was drowned.

How to get there:

Hermitage Castle is located one mile off the B6399, which runs between Hawick and Newcastleton - follow the brown information signs to the castle. It is also accessible from the A7 which is the main route between Hawick and Carlisle. The castle is under the ownership of Historic Environment Scotland, is open seasonally (April - October), and has an admission charge.

10. Old Roxburgh Castle

What you'll discover:

Having been born and brought up in Kelso, I'd often get on my bike and go with friends on mini adventures around the local area - Old Roxburgh Castle was often our destination of choice. As a child my imagination would run wild when discovering the ruins of this medieval castle; I'd always be armed with my sword (made from the finest recently discovered dry branch of course).

The medieval castle was originally built by the Scots on the narrow neck of land between the Rivers Tweed and Teviot, upstream from the town of Kelso. It is thought by some that there may have been a Dark Age fort located here prior to the castle's construction but no physical evidence exists today of the earlier structure. It was positioned to give the best possible protection to the thriving town/city of Roxburgh, where Scotland's first royal mint was located. Roxburgh's wealth and importance meant that it was desired by both Scots and English alike - this is one of the reasons the castle changed hands ten times or more between the two nations.

On one occasion in early 1314, the loyal right hand man of King Robert the Bruce, the audacious and cunning Sir James Douglas (featured in treasure number 71) managed to take the castle by getting his men to disguise themselves as cows (cows were much smaller in those days) and on reaching the southern ramparts unnoticed, scaled the walls and took the English completely by surprise.

The castle suffered major destruction in the aftermath of a siege by King James II of Scotland in 1460 (during this siege James was mortally wounded by his own cannon whilst trying to fix a blockage in its barrel) and thus it could no longer be used by the English as a staging post for further invasions. There was a brief period of reoccupation by English forces in 1545 for five years during the rough wooing, during which time the castle was made usable, however no proper reconstruction took place. After this time the castle was fully dismantled and abandoned. What you see today are the great mounds that were built to elevate the castle above the two rivers, and some large fragments of stonework from the walls.

It is wonderful to wander around the top and get a sense of the place and its history. Take a moment (and maybe even a picnic) and enjoy the views looking north over the Tweed towards Floors Castle, the largest inhabited stately home in Scotland.

How to get there:

The ruin sits on the A699 road that runs between Kelso and Maxton. Park next to the Teviot Bridge on the opposite side of Springwood Caravan Park and walk a short distance along the north bank of the River Teviot.

11. Fatlips Castle

What you'll discover:

The name 'Fatlips' may seem a very odd name for a castle but it is said to have derived from the welcome you received from the owners, the Turnbulls of Cragside. Not that they gave you a fat lip from a hefty thump from their fists, but the very opposite; the name Fatlips apparently comes from their overly welcoming ways where ladies received lots of big kisses - given the history of the Border area this in itself stands out as odd!

The castle is a fantastic example of a Borders Tower House. Tower Houses were at one time a common sight right across the Border Country and are directly related to the turbulent history previously mentioned. They would have been bitterly fought over and were the sites of many a bloody battle or skirmish. The majority of these towers were destroyed on the command of King James the VI of Scotland (James I of England) so that they could not be used against him, or get in the way of his pacifying of the Border Country. After taking charge of both Kingdoms James wished to create a greater sense of unity; no longer was there to be a fractious, dangerous and divided society which had become the norm for the Border folk. During this time of 'pacification' many were forced to leave in what are referred to as (but not often talked or written about) the Border Clearances. The people were dispersed (in most cases it was forced rather than voluntary) across a vast area; many went to continental Europe and became traders or highly valued mercenaries, others travelled west to the province of Ulster in the north of Ireland to settle as part of King James's plantation/colonisation project. In time these settlers became known as Ulster-Scots and in the early eighteenth century many moved on again to America, mostly to Pennsylvania initially before venturing further inland and south. These Ulster-Scots become known as Scots-Irish. The descendents of these people continued with their frontier spirit of going beyond and into the unknown - it is no surprise that the first man on the moon was a certain Neil Armstrong who can trace his ancestry back to the Borders to a breed of tough, hardy and resourceful frontier people. Was the first man on the moon American or an exile Borderer? I like to think the latter.

To access the castle you have to walk up the quite steep footpath from the road - it can be a bit slippy especially after rain so reasonable footwear is recommended. A torch is also advisable as there is no lighting in the tower. On arrival and once inside you can look out from the ramparts and enjoy three hundred and sixty degree views of the surrounding Scottish Borders countryside. It is easy to get a sense of what life must have been like living in such a place and the feelings of terror when at dawn you heard the sound of hundreds of horses' hooves in the distance thundering towards your home, or seeing the flickering firelight from torches and getting ready for them coming your way.

How to get there:

Firstly you will need to visit Oliver's Garage in Denholm to get the key for the castle - it's located on the far side of the village green opposite the main road. You pay a deposit of £10 and on return of the key you get £5 back. Be aware the garage is closed on Sundays. You can still explore the outside of the tower for free but to get inside the key is essential. From Denholm take the B6405 for Hassendean and once over the River Teviot take an immediate right and follow the road for approximately three miles. Park opposite the small wooden sign, and then follow the path to the tower.

12. Dollar Glen/Castle Campbell

What you'll discover:

Dollar is not where the currency originated (the Kingdom of Bohemia apparently) but it does beg the question - where does the word 'Dollar' come from? As with a lot of place names in Scotland there is often more than one explanation. However, in a historical context the location of the village falls within an area that was predominantly P-Celtic, Brythonic/Pictish speaking. Thus, the name likely means 'an area of arable land/fields' or 'a high/steep valley'. Given the surrounding landscape both interpretations are plausible. Dollar is one of a series of villages referred to as the Hillfoots due to their location at the foot of the Ochil Hills, and it is into these hills that we venture.

There are two burns, the Burn of Care and the Burn of Sorrow, that come together to form part of the Kelly Burn that runs through modern day Dollar. Upstream, these burns have cut neat and narrow gorges and it is in between these two gorges that Castle Campbell impressively sits. Originally called 'Castle Gloom' - but before your mind begins conjuring up images of swirling fog and the painful screeching of some malnourished beast - the name in fact comes from the Gaelic word 'glom' meaning chasm. Although there would have been an earlier fortification from at least the twelfth century, what you can see now mostly dates from 1430.

The castle was built by John Stewart (Lord Lorn) but fell into Campbell hands with the marriage of Colin Campbell to John's daughter Isabel in 1465. Later that century in 1488 Colin Campbell successfully petitioned King James IV to have the name changed to Castle Campbell. The location of the castle gave the famous Clan Campbell chiefs relatively easy access to wherever the King of Scotland was in residence, usually Stirling Castle or Edinburgh Castle.

For the best and fullest experience, park in the village and follow the Kelly Burn upstream until the path splits in two. One side takes you on a lovely walk through mature oak trees; on the other side you follow the path which takes you into the lush, green, almost tropical-like, steep-sided gorges created by the burns. Although Castle Campbell is distinctly Scottish in appearance with its rectangular keep with defensive barmkin walls, it does also have a bit of continental influence in that there is a 'loggia', an open walkway usually found in warmer climates, incorporated into its design. In the garden there is a spot referred to as 'John Knox's Pulpit' where the firebrand preacher gave a sermon in 1556. When visiting the castle make the effort to get to the top parapet because the views looking down the glen and beyond are very impressive. Dollar Glen and Castle Campbell are the sort of places where once visited are never forgotten.

How to get there:

Dollar is located on the main road that takes you between Stirling to St Andrews (the A91). Follow signs for the castle and park on either side of the Kelly Burn. You can drive closer to the castle by following the Castle Road. The castle is in the ownership of Historic Environment Scotland, open all year round, and has an admission charge.

13. Loch Leven Castle

What you'll discover:

For lovers of Mary Queen of Scots, Loch Leven Castle is a must. Located on one of the larger islands found in Loch Leven, the castle dates back to the fourteenth century and for the most part it was in the hands of the Douglas family. It was a very strategically placed castle being located between Edinburgh and Perth. Mary was taken here in June 1567 as a prisoner following her defeat at the Battle of Carberry Hill. Part of her terms of surrender was that she would not be imprisoned, but she was sadly betrayed by her rebellious noblemen. This was not her first visit to the castle as she had been there two years previously as a guest of Sir William Douglas of Loch Leven in which instance she had been welcomed and treated with respect (well, apart from meeting with the leading Calvinist John Knox, who, let's be honest, wasn't one for engaging in light conversation with Catholics, especially female ones with French mannerisms - Queen or no Queen!).

On her second and far less enjoyable visit she remained a prisoner for eleven months. During her time in captivity she had a miscarriage of twins brought on by a fever following her imprisonment. She was also forced to sign abdication papers handing her crown over to her infant son James. In time she managed a daring escape aided by George Douglas (brother of William) who was besotted with Mary, and by incorporating the help of a young orphaned member of the family called Willie, she dressed as a servant and made good her escape.

The location, surrounding scenery, and history of Loch Leven Castle combine to make this a treasure. When you travel over to the island to visit there is something tragically romantic about following in the footsteps of one of the best known figures from Scotland's past; to ponder what must have been going through Mary's mind following the deceitful behaviour of her nobles given that they had promised not to imprison her and yet, here she was on her way to her internment.

If you are remaining in the area for any length of time and fancy stretching your legs there is a thirteen mile circular loop walk that takes you around the loch. Make sure to visit Loch Leven's Larder, a restaurant/shop/delicatessen for quality refuelling.

How to get there:

Take the exit off the M90 motorway at Junction 6 for Kinross, and follow the brown information signs for Loch Leven Castle. Park at the jetty and buy your tickets at the small ticket office. The castle is in the care of Historic Environment Scotland and is open seasonally - please call ahead to check the sailings and book your seat on the boat.

14. Dun Da-Lamh Pictish Fort

What you'll discover:

If ever there was a perfect site for a strategic viewpoint Dun Da-Lamh is it. It translates into the 'Fort of the two hands', possibly relating to the two peaks next to each other where the fort is located. It sits atop a rocky precipice, has an incredibly commanding position, and must have taken a momentous amount of effort to construct. It is only when you get up close do you realise that there is such a substantial fortification here at all which is why so few people know about it.

This Iron Age Pictish fort is testament to the skills of the Pictish people who build it given that it has walls up to seven metres thick, some of which are still standing in a relatively well preserved state. From a distance this place would have oozed power. It was obviously an important place and would have been known throughout the land; this would have helped with the status of whoever occupied the fort.

It was built to overlook the junction between Glen Shira and the River Spey to the north and east, and Strathmashie and the River Mashie to the south. Although the site has been surveyed by archaeologists, it has never been excavated so who knows what artifacts or stories lie, as yet untold, beneath the layers of rubble, earth and mosses. It is also interesting to ponder that if the lands constituting Pictland covered everything north of the Rivers Forth and Clyde, Dun Da-Lamh was thus almost right in the middle of that

Kingdom, making it a possible ancient Pictish Capital. Most scholars say the heartland of the Picts was much further to the east - this could well be true given the number and density of carved Pictish standing stones you find in that area, but that may just have been their 'spiritual' heartland and not the site of governance (much in the same way that for centuries St Andrews on the east coast was the religious focus of Scotland yet the governing capital was Stirling situated in the middle of the central lowlands). Only with proper archaeological excavation will we learn the true purpose of Dun Da-Lamh.

Take a walk up, enjoy a flask of something warm whilst looking out over the amazing landscape, and ponder for yourself the significance of this treasure.

How to get there:

Park in the Pattack Falls Nature Trail car park on the A86 and walk a short distance along the road in the direction of Newtonmore (please take care when walking along the road), then turn left on a forestry track. The walk is marked but you are generally going in the direction of Newtonmore before you begin to climb up towards the fort. Be aware that sometimes your route is diverted due to forestry operations.

15. Kilchurn Castle

What you'll discover:

If you want that picture-postcard image to show all your friends of a ruined Scottish castle then Kilchurn Castle fits the bill perfectly. Originally built in the style of a traditional Scottish Tower House by Sir Colin Campbell, Lord of Glenorchy, in the mid fifteenth century, it was constructed on a rocky island at the east end of Loch Awe, where the River Orchy flows into the loch. Loch Awe is the longest loch in Scotland at twenty-five miles. Today getting to the castle involves a fairly straightforward walk along a spit of land that connects the castle to the main shore, however originally access was either by some form of hidden causeway - not dissimilar to how ancient crannogs were accessed many centuries before - or by boat. The land connection to the shore occurred for two reasons; firstly the loch level was dropped slightly in 1817, and secondly layers of silt have built up from the mouth of the River Orchy.

Although the location is highly defensive and has a high status element to it, there is also a lot of symbolism at work too. The castle is situated below the mountain Ben Cruachan, which was deemed to be right in the very heartland of Clan Campbell country. The Campbell's battle cry was 'Cruachan Cruachan' - shouting the name of the mountain reminded all Campbell combatants of where they were from and belonged. By locating the castle below the mountain it emphasised that the Clan Chief was right at the heart of his lands and people.

The Campbell's gained the lands around Loch Awe from the MacDougall's following their loyal support of King Robert the Bruce in the Wars of Independence in the early fourteenth century. As for Kilchurn Castle itself, it remained in use until the mid eighteenth century when eventually it was abandoned due to being struck and partially destroyed by lightning. As you walk into the castle you can see the remnants of the damage done where a turret collapsed. It is worth going to the viewing platform on the top of the tower to read the information boards and to admire the views.

How to get there:

Access to the castle is by foot or bicycle only, although there is some basic parking for vehicles just north of the junction between the A819 to Inveraray from the A85, where a track veers off down a steep slope. The footpath takes you under the railway. Access is free but not always possible - check with Historic Environment Scotland, custodians of the castle, before visiting.

16. Dunadd Hill Fort

What you'll discover:

The Scots as a people originate from the north coast of Ireland in what is today County Antrim; they seemed to enjoy rain so decided to follow the large dark rain clouds that swept over the North Channel from west to east and sailed over in pursuit around 500 CE (or possibly before). There has been some discussion over the years regarding the origins of the name 'Scot'. It seems most likely to derive from the Latin 'Scotti' meaning pirate/raider, or possibly trader. The Latin also gives us the word 'Scotia' to describe their Kingdom, however the Scots named their land - which constituted much of the west coast of Scotland *and* the north coast of Ireland -' Dál Riata', possibly relating to the name of an individual. The North Channel between what is today Ireland and Scotland was not viewed as an obstacle by these seafaring people but as a highway. Dál Riata constituted most of what we refer to today as Argyll. Interestingly the word Argyll means the 'coast of the Gael', referring to the connection of the Scots to the Gaels and of course the culture and language they brought with them from Ireland.

The Scots established their power base at Dunadd - it was an incredibly well defended place with various rings of thick defensive walls surrounded on all sides by a low lying bog area. Within this Dark Age fortress, there is archaeological evidence indicating that gold-working was taking place and this evidence tells us that Dunadd was a place of very high culture and status. Time has taken its toll on Dunadd and it is hard to make out where the defensive walls would have been - thankfully the information board in the car park has a helpful illustration. On top of the site today there is a relatively flat rock, with a carved footprint very similar to that of the print found at Dunino

Den (as mentioned in treasure number 68). The footprint was very symbolic; when a new King was crowned they stepped into the footprint, literally following in the footsteps of those who had come before. As the new King you were to endeavour to emulate your predecessors good and considerate leadership, you were expected to be at one with the earth, and hopefully under your Kingship the land would be fruitful and your people would thrive. This way of thinking was not in any way unique to the Scots or the Picts because there are foot carvings to be found across much of Europe, proving that there were common threads of thinking amongst the ancient peoples.

It is just brilliant to scramble and find your way to the top, walk in the footsteps of ancient Kings, and to look out over the ancient landscape beyond.

How to get there:

Dunadd is located a short distance from the main Kilmartin to Lochgilphead A816 road and is signposted.

17. Carnasserie Castle

What you'll discover:

Carnasserie Castle is one of the very few castles that you find from sixteenth century Scotland that was not built with defence in mind first. It was always intended to be more of a grand residence, a status symbol, although some defensive design was still necessary given the unsettled times. Construction was started in 1565 by the reforming churchman John Carswell (also referred to as 'the Bishop Carswell' with no hint of irony given that the Calvinist Church did away with traditional church hierarchical structure). Carswell is famous because he was the first person to actually publish a printed book in Scots Gaelic - a translation of John Knox's Book of Common Order - which was to be used by the Reformed Church of Scotland. By translating the book it made it easier to convert Gaelic-speaking people away from Catholicism and towards Protestantism. Carswell died in 1572 so he didn't get much of a chance to enjoy his grand surroundings of Carnasserie.

In the following years the castle changed hands a couple of times but eventually was blown up by Royalist forces in 1685 after the owner at the time rose against James VII/II, and it was never properly repaired. To be honest as castles go it had a fairly short lifespan.

As you enter the old studded door on the north-side you begin to discover the castle through what would have been the vaulted stores. Then explore the levels above, eventually leading you higher and higher up the spiral staircase until you arrive at the roof viewpoint which gives you brilliant views looking south down Kilmartin Glen. The best thing about visiting the castle is that there are usually very few people there at any one time, so it is unlikely to be busy. There is a walled section on the south side which is quite protected from the wind where it is good to have a picnic. Carnasserie Castle is a great addition whilst visiting this area - it does not disappoint.

How to get there:

Carnasserie Castle is two miles north of Kilmartin on the A816 before the junction with the B840 which takes you on a lovely drive along the south side of Loch Awe. There is a good gravel car park, so simply park and walk up the track to the castle which you'll see above you. There is no admission charge. Whilst in the area it is worth trying to explore Kilmartin Glen as fully as you can, discussed more in treasures 16 and 77.

18. Castle Moil

What you'll discover:

Castle Moil occupies a commanding position overlooking the deep narrow strait (or kyle) between the Isle of Skye and the mainland at Kyle of Lochalsh, near the village of Kyleakin. The name of the village relates to King Haakon of Norway (there were four King Haakon's in total) dating back to the tenth century with references to a castle located there named at various times Dunakin, Dun Haakon or Dun Akyn. The castle's position was important in order to watch and monitor passing ships choosing to travel the more sheltered route of the Sound of Raasay, through the Kyle of Lochalsh, along the edge of Loch Duich and then into Kylerhea at the south of Skye, rather than the more exposed and perilous Minch on the west side of Skye.

Dunakin, which became Castle Moil (meaning the 'bare castle'), was the seat of Clan MacKinnon who acquired the castle in the tenth century through marriage of the chief's son Findanus to a Norwegian Princess called Mary. In local folklore it is suggested that Mary and Findanus ran a heavy chain (or more likely a thick rope or net) across the Kyle to prevent ships from passing unless they paid a toll. It is also said that if the sailors paid a bit more than the requested toll, Mary would bare her naked chest - to what would have been a fairly sexually frustrated bunch of men. This behaviour earned Mary the prefix of 'saucy' and thereafter she was referred to as 'Saucy Mary'.

The narrow strait was also where King Haakon IV rested his fleet in 1263 before travelling down the west coast to meet and be beaten by Alexander III of Scotland in the Battle of Largs. The aftermath of the battle led to the treaty of Perth in 1266 where it was agreed that the Western Isles and the northern mainland of Scotland, which had been under Norse rule for centuries, would come under the rule of the Scottish King.

Today the castle ruins that you see are mostly from the fifteenth century, and originally it would have been a fairly impressive three storey castle with a basement which would have been used for storage and possibly a kitchen. Despite the castle being easily seen and relatively easy to get to it is rarely visited so if you are in no particular hurry it is worth stopping by to visit; there's a good chance you might spot an otter or two.

On the tenth of October 2010 there was a very surprising and unexpected visit in the form of one of the British Government's nuclear deterrent Trident submarines, much to the alarm of the local population. HMS Astute ran aground whilst on a "secret" training exercise much to embarrassment of the British Navy and the Ministry of Defence. Thankfully no harm was done except to a few submariner's egos.

How to get there:

Once in the village of Kyleakin on the Isle of Skye, park in the car park near the King Haakon Bar. On the opposite side of the green you will see a row of houses, business premises and Saucy Mary's pub. Walk to the far end and over a small bridge to South Obbe Road. Follow the road to the end and thereafter follow the track to the ruined castle. Be careful of the tides...and unexpected submarines!

19. Dunnottar Castle

What you'll discover:

Dunnottar is a corruption of 'Dun Fhoithear' which means the 'fort of the shelving' or 'falling slope' in Gaelic. It is one of the most spectacular castles ruins in Scotland. At this point I must admit a bias towards Dunnottar Castle because much of what you see today was put there by the Keith Clan, which is my own family heritage. Putting my bias aside, Dunnottar Castle is a seriously impressive place. On arrival you are met with an incredible visual spectacle of the ruined castle atop a rocky peninsula. As you walk down the path to gain access, it becomes even more impressive and thoughts move onto the effort required to build on this location. The rock is four hundred and forty million year old conglomerate, and on first appearance looks like fused-together gravel that would just break away and disappear but of course this is not the case - it is incredibly hard-wearing. It is also known as 'pudding stone' as it resembles a fruitcake.

Archaeologists say that the first structures would have been simple, early Christian buildings established by St Ninian, an early missionary amongst the Pictish peoples of the north east of Scotland. By the time it was attacked and destroyed in the ninth century by the Vikings it had become a well established and great fortress.

Through the Middle Ages it played an important role in many major historical events including the Wars of Independence, where it was captured and held by the English only for William Wallace to re-take and destroy it so that it couldn't be used again as a staging post for further English invasion. During the War of the Three Kingdoms (also referred to as the English Civil War) Oliver Cromwell laid siege to the now rebuilt castle for nine months. He wanted the Crown Jewels of Scotland (also known as the 'Honours of Scotland') that were being kept safe inside, but alas when the siege finally succeeded and the Cromwellian soldiers gained access, they found no crown jewels. They had already been smuggled out months earlier right under the English soldier's noses, via either a straw laden cart or lowered down the cliffs to an awaiting boat, after which they were buried under the floor of nearby Kinnef Church.

In 1685 the castle was used as a prison for Covenanters mostly from the south west of Scotland. The prisoners were kept in squalid unsanitary conditions, not receiving the kind of hospitality that I'd normally associate with my family… some prisoners died and others who tried to escape were cruelly tortured. It was a very poor show by the Keith clan in my opinion and a low point in the family history.

Although the castle has seen a fair bit of violence over the years, life wasn't always turbulent and within its rocky confines not too unpleasant, there was even time for games like bowls. With such impressive vistas and history you'll be hard pushed not to be moved by this amazing place.

How to get there:

Dunnottar Castle is located two miles south of Stonehaven. From the A90 turn off for Stonehaven onto the A92 and follow the signs to the castle from there. There is an admission charge to visit the castle, payable on arrival.

Beauty spots

It is the beauty, splendour and variety of Scotland's landscapes that attract so many people here. From wild and raw to soft and mellow Scotland has something for everyone.

20. St Abb's Head and Coldingham Bay

What you'll discover:

The origin of the name 'St Abbs' goes way back into the dim and distant past - the early seventh century to be exact. Aebbe was the daughter of King Aethelfrith of Bernicia - Bernicia was an Anglian Kingdom that covered much of what is today south east Scotland and north east England.

It was during a time of war with Deira, a Kingdom to the south of Bernicia, that Aebbe and her family fled in exile to the Kingdom of Dál Riata in the west, ruled by King Eochaid Buide. Whilst in the west, Aebbe converted to Christianity and once her family returned to power in the east they brought with them their newly found faith. Aebbe established a monastery near what is today known as St Abb's Head.

Although the monastery established by Aebbe burned down after her death, her name remains. The coastline at St Abb's Head is stunning and is a haven for many species of sea bird, as well as a healthy population of seals. The rugged cliffs are fascinating due to the different sedimentary and volcanic rock types to be found. The rocks are so fascinating that just up the coast at Siccar Point (near Cockburnspath) James Hutton, who is referred to as the founder of modern geology, demonstrated his theory of rock unconformity which he had also witnessed on the Isle of Arran, Jedburgh, and at Salisbury Crags in Edinburgh. The sea area around the cliffs is now part of a National Nature Reserve and it's worth taking a walk along the cliffs looking back to the village to really enjoy this special place. You can do a circular route to a lighthouse but make sure you have appropriate footwear and clothing.

A short distance south of St Abb's is the lovely village of Coldingham, which has a secluded beach, a popular spot for surfing. Near the beach are the remains of Coldingham Priory which was established by the Benedictine Order, and well worth a look around. There are some interesting Templar gravestones on display as well as information boards to help with interpretation. In the village there are a few options for sustenance and libations should you be requiring them after your walk or just fancy a pit stop.

How to get there:

From the A1 road heading either north or south you can take the A1107 or the B6438 to the coast. St Abb's and Coldingham are well sign-posted. The easiest thing to do is park at the St Abb's visitor centre and explore from there.

21. Rumbling Brig (bridge)

What you'll discover:

There are two Rumbling Brigs in Scotland and they are located not that far apart from each other. One is found on the River Braan near to Dunkeld, north of Perth - it is a lovely spot and also worth a visit. However our Rumbling Brig is located in a steep gorge on the River Devon near to the village of Crook of Devon. The name would suggest that there is only one bridge; however there are three river crossings built on top of one another. The first is nothing more than a rudimentary stone slab - not a bridge as such but it still serves the purpose of connecting the two sides of the gorge. The first properly engineered and designed bridge dates from 1713. However by the 1800s this bridge was deemed inadequate and an additional bridge was built above it. Completed in 1816, this final bridge remains in use today.

The river is liable to flooding and even after a small amount of rain the water can turn into a raging torrent, creating the rumbling sound which of course gives its name to the place. The gorge is quite special for Helen and I as it was one of the first places I took her for a date. I am not known for my romantic tendencies but the beautiful walk coupled with the impressive gorge and a picnic must have been a winning combination because Helen stayed with me and decided that I was a keeper. It was a lovely sunny day and we walked in a loop around the gorge - unfortunately this is no longer possible as the upper timber bridge that enabled the walk to be a loop got washed away some years back - that said it is still worth a visit.

How to get there:

The hamlet of Rumbling Bridge is located on the A823, which is accessible from the A977 and the A91. Park in the layby south of the bridge itself and walk into the gorge from there.

22. Wormistoune House and Gardens

What you'll discover:

Tucked away in the East Neuk of the Kingdom of Fife, Wormistoune House and Gardens is a wee oasis of colour, nature and history in what is an arable and heavily-farmed, yet pleasant, landscape. Within its small thirteen acre confines you will find an early seventeenth century house that has being fully restored, externally at least at the time of writing, with incredible attention to detail and use of traditional skills. You'll also find a walled garden that has been brought back to life filled with colour and interest, the creation of a lochan which provides habitat for all sorts of animals and wildlife, and there are further plans to bring much of the rest of the grounds, including the old doocot (dovecot) back into use.

I have to admit I am not the biggest visitor of manmade well-groomed gardens - for me they curtail nature and are an example of humans bending nature to our will - but Wormistoune is different. The project to bring this small, old (dating back to 1180) estate back to life has been a labour of love and persistence by its owners James and Gemma McCallum over decades, with the help and advice from their head gardener Katherine Taylor. Nothing is overstated; there is a warmth not only from the buildings and garden but also from the people. I took my mum there after she'd had an operation to help raise her spirits and it worked brilliantly - everyone was very welcoming and took time to chat with us. Something else that also makes a difference is that the money charged to visit (£5 per person) is donated to a cancer charity called Maggie's, which James is involved in.

The whole experience was a real treat and it is well worth making the effort to go and visit. Although Wormistoune welcomes visitors all year round it is best to visit when most of the flowers are in bloom during the main summer months.

How to get there:

Wormistoune House is located a short distance off the A917 between Crail and St Andrews. From Crail you travel approximately one mile north and then turn right, or if travelling from St Andrews travel approximately two miles south of Kingsbarns and turn left. Visits are by appointment only or on one of the house's open days. To visit contact the head gardener by email Ktaylor.home@googlemail.com

23. Corrieshalloch Gorge

What you'll discover:

As you travel from Easter Ross into Wester Ross en route to Ullapool in the north west of Scotland, you are driving through a wild and unforgiving landscape yet beautiful at the same time. Near Ullapool you must visit the Corrieshalloch Gorge with the Falls of Measach because you are rewarded with an absolute feast for the eyes. An American friend once said to me when visiting "the Corrieshalloch Gorge is no Grand Canyon!" and I responded by saying "no, although the Grand Canyon makes a good second place!"

The gorge is a great example of a box canyon - one of the best in the whole of Scotland. For such a beautiful place it seems odd that the name translates into 'the ugly/unattractive cauldron/hollow' where the 'corrie' part of the name relates to the word cauldron. It just goes to show how perceptions of beauty change over the years.

When you arrive you have to walk down a short winding path and then you are met with a small bridge that takes you right over the Falls of Measach ('place of the platters'). You can just feel the energy rising up from the falls crashing forty-five metres below. I have to be honest and admit to a fear of heights and this fear just adds to the whole feel of the place. Once on the other side of the bridge there is a short walk down to a cantilevered viewing platform which again doesn't help the old vertigo, but is definitely worth 'the heebie jeebies' (the jitters) for the views.

How to get there:

The gorge is easy to find being located just off the main road to Ullapool from Inverness, beyond the junction between the A832 and A835 road to Dundonald. There is now a new parking area with a fee. Corrieshalloch Gorge is looked after by the National Trust for Scotland and the money goes towards upkeep and repairs. There were some major works on the bridge done back between 2010 and 2012 so the donation is used wisely.

24. Loch Morar and silver sands

What you'll discover:

For many visitors to Scotland Loch Ness is on their bucket list of 'must see things'. Loch Ness is nice I admit but we're looking for something a bit more special. Loch Morar and its environs have that something special. Firstly the surrounding scenery is dramatic to say the least with words like rugged, raw and atmospheric tripping off the tongue without even engaging the brain. Loch Morar is the deepest body of freshwater in Scotland with a maximum depth of three hundred and ten metres. The water in the loch is very clear, unlike most lochs which are very dark in colour due to the peaty soil, not so good for food to feed the habitat but pleasant on the eye. Due to its location on the west coast, it has far fewer visitors than places like Loch Ness or Loch Lomond, but it is still easy enough to get to, meaning you can really enjoy the tranquillity here without the crowded coach tours arriving to disturb your peace and quiet.

The road you drive to get to Loch Morar is referred to as the 'Road to the Isles' from Fort William to Mallaig, and is one of the most enjoyable and scenic roads to travel on in Scotland. The river that flows from Loch Morar into Morar Bay is one of the shortest rivers in Scotland at just short of a mile in length (depending on the tide), and drops a height of only nine metres from the mouth of the river to where it enters the bay. Over the years, the River Morar has deposited soft and very light coloured sand, which has created lovely small beaches on the bay, referred to as the 'silver sands'. Beyond the sands you start to get into the rocks of the main coastline and it was here that my father and I went mussel-picking many years ago. We took them back to our lodgings and once cooked they were the best mussels I have ever eaten, some of them even had small light grey coloured pearls in them so be careful if you decide to do the same. Welcome to the wild west coast of Scotland!

How to get there:

Finding Loch Morar couldn't be easier. Simply drive on the A830 from Fort William (the Road to the Isles) and Loch Morar is in between Arisaig and Mallaig (where you take the ferry to the Isle of Skye and the Small Isles).

25. Bealach Na Ba

What you'll discover:

The Bealach Na Ba or 'pass of the cow' is the highest road in Scotland, travelling between Applecross and Shieldaig in the north west. From the top of the pass on a clear day the three hundred and sixty degree views of the surrounding landscape are frankly jaw-dropping. To the south you'll see the mountains of Moidart and Knoydart, to the east the Torridon range, to the north the Sound of Rhona, and to the west you can pick out much of the eastern coastline of the Isle of Skye, with both the Black and Red Cuillin mountains in view.

The name of this pass dates back to a time when much of the Scottish economy, more particularly in the Highlands but everywhere to a greater or lesser degree, was based around the breeding, rearing and selling of cows. There were well established cattle driving routes called 'drove roads' that crisscrossed the landscape throughout the Highlands, Lowlands and then on through the Borders into England, for it was England that many of the beasts were eventually destined. It took a particularly hardy breed of men (and they *were* all men before you call me sexist) called 'drovers' to undertake the task of buying, driving and selling the cattle, with many risks and hardships on the way to contend with. To name but a few, the unpredictable weather, unsavoury characters en route, and the midges (tiny biting flies), must have been a nightmare to deal with. All this was the norm for the drovers and there was no guarantee of any profit at the end of it all. Many of the drove roads would lead to the main cattle 'trysts' (markets) in the Central Lowlands of Scotland such as Crieff, Perth, Stirling and Falkirk. By the time the drovers arrived at the trysts the numbers of cattle in a driven herd could amount into the thousands.

The drove roads weren't just for the driving of cows as they also served as a way of bringing news, and many of the drove roads even had their own folklore, characters and stories. It is quite something to stand at the top of the Bealach and imagine for a moment the sight and sound of a sizable herd of cows slowly winding their way up the hill side, plus the cries and calls of the drovers who were trying to keep the cattle on track as they slowly travelled up from Applecross, over the pass and onto Loch Kishorn, Shieldaig and beyond. For many of us today life is relatively easy, as we have the time to stop and enjoy the scenery. For the drovers of old they would have maybe paused for a moment to catch their breath, but they had a job to do, and as they would have looked south admiring the scene there would have been the knowledge that this was only the beginning of a long hard journey still to come.

How to get there:

The Bealach Na Ba is located between the village of Applecross and the main A896. The road has many tight hairpin bends (switchbacks) so before driving this road ensure that your vehicle has good brakes. Whilst in Applecross, the Applecross Inn offers high quality pub food.

26. Fortingall Yew Tree

What you'll discover:

When it comes to old living things in Scotland the Fortingall Yew tree tops the list. Estimates vary as to the exact age of the tree; some experts say it is between two to three thousand years old with others saying possibly five thousand years old and beyond. It may well be that the current tree is about three thousand years old but the same living organism has been there for five thousand years or more. With these kinds of impressive numbers you might think that this tree would be enormous - it did once have a huge trunk but it was damaged by fire, so what stands today is far smaller. For its protection there is now a wall and railings around the tree. It is astonishing to think that a single living organism can live for so long.

The path to the tree has landmark historic events carved into the slabs, which help to put some kind of context into what this tree has lived through - from the Bronze Age, through the Wars of Independence, to the moon landings and beyond. The reason it has lasted so long is because of the species itself - yew trees tend to live between five and six hundred years - anything beyond that falls into the rare bracket. Even if the Fortingall Yew is 'only' two thousand years old, it is still one of the oldest living organisms in Europe.

To the ancient pre-Christian people of Scotland a yew tree was steeped in myth and lore. It is said that in these times a yew tree would be planted over a person's grave so that the roots would wind their way down through the corpse, push out the eyes and hold the skeleton in place to stop the dead from rising. You will often find yew trees in Kirk (church) yards for two reasons; one spiritual, one practical. The spiritual side relates to the cycle of life, death and rebirth; as the older growth branches break off due to weight of the foliage or just age, instead of disease getting into the open fracture and killing the tree, new shoots will grow from it and the tree will continue to live. Within a Christian context this represents the death and subsequent resurrection of Christ. From the practical point of view, the yew tree acted as a deterrent to stop herdsmen from allowing their stock to wander into a graveyard to graze. Because most of the yew tree is poisonous, if cows were to eat the leaves either dead from the ground or alive from the tree itself, the animals would certainly get ill if not die.

There is a small hotel at Fortingall if you fancy popping in for a quick refreshment, and a mile or so to the east there are standing stones to be explored.

How to get there:

There are two ways to approach Fortingall; either travel from Aberfeldy on the B846 and turn left when you see the signpost or alternatively you can travel on the A827 which follows the shores of Loch Tay and then turn up to the left when you reach Fearnan.

27. Glen Orchy Falls

What you'll discover:

Glen Orchy is a short glen (valley) of only eleven miles in length from Bridge of Orchy on the A82 down to Dalmally. It was in this secluded glen that well known Scottish folk hero Rob Roy MacGregor's mother was born (she was a Campbell incidentally). Thanks to its seclusion, even today you can find remnants of what was Scotland's great Caledonian Pine Forest, a forest that would have - at a time before humans arrived - covered almost the entire area that now constitutes the geographical Highlands. This once great forest has gradually disappeared over the years, and had the First World War not ended when it did it would have been completely wiped out all together, due to the volume of timber required. In the years after 1918, efforts were made to reforest many upland areas of Scotland, but rather than using the indigenous slow-growing Scots Pine, the fast-growing Norway spruce was favoured. These tree plantations still make up the bulk of Scotland's forests, covering approximately fifteen percent of Scotland's land mass, as opposed to three percent which is native woodland. Today there are renewed efforts to reforest, but the lessons of old have been learned and only native species are being used. With the return of indigenous trees and forests we are also beginning to see the reintroduction of more of Scotland's native animals as well, such as beavers and birds of prey.

The water that has timelessly flowed down Glen Orchy has hollowed out beautiful circular shapes in the rock (sometimes referred to as 'witches'

cauldrons') - the bubbling and spilling of the water adds to the effect of the place. During heavy rain the river can become like an eleven mile funnel of white-water and there are those who are brave enough to go rafting down the river when it is in flood. I once met a New Zealander (who happened to be from Scottish ancestry) who had rafted all over the world on some of the largest and most dangerous rivers to be found, but it was on his trip down the River Orchy whilst in spate that he almost lost his life. He said it was Mother Earth's way of telling him that he'd had a good run and had his fun but it was his time to stop...thankfully he listened and has never rafted again.

It's worth stopping for a while, finding a dry spot on the exposed rocks to just sit, watch and listen to the water below.

How to get there:

The Glen Orchy Falls are half way along the B8074 which runs from the A82 at Bridge of Orchy to Dalmally on the A85. Stop when you see a bridge that crosses the river than can be driven over - the falls are just upstream from the bridge.

28. Glen Lonan (Road of the Kings)

What you'll discover:

Whether you're travelling to or from Oban, the drive down Glen Lonan is worth a detour. The route starts (or finishes) at Taynuilt. It is a lovely single track road that meanders its way through the glen but what makes it so magical are the ancient cairns and standing stones that you pass on the way. The folklore that surrounds the glen gives it the name the 'Road of the Kings', relating to the route taken by a King on his final journey to his resting place on the Isle of Iona.

From the ninth (at least) to the eleventh centuries, it is said that all of Scotland's Kings were buried on the sacred Isle of Iona (treasure number 7), Kings such as Kenneth MacAlpin, Aed, Giric, Constantine I and their many successors. The procession made its way to Loch Feochan, a sea loch which feeds into the Firth of Lorn. Interestingly on the shore of Loch Feochan is a rock known as Carraig nam Marbh, the 'Rock of the Dead'. It was from this natural jetty that the King would have made his last voyage by sea across the Firth of Lorn, along and round the Ross of Mull to Iona. For me this brings to mind the legend of King Arthur where he was taken over the western sea to the sacred Isle of Avalon.

The name and the accompanying folklore are fascinating, but the cairns and standing stones would have been put in place by a far more ancient society long before any Dark Age and early Medieval Kings had even passed through the glen. This indicates that in some way this beautiful and ancient land has always had a very sacred feel about it. Take your time and stop often - you may have to because there are Highland Cows and sheep that often wander on the road.

How to get there:

From Oban you need to travel past the Rugby Club and continue following signs for Taynuilt. If travelling on the A85 from the east, when you get to Taynuilt you'll take the first proper turning on the left at the Taynuilt Hotel and follow the sign that says Glen Lonan.

29. Easdale (Isle of Seil) and Isle of Easdale

What you'll discover:

To get to the Isle of Seil and therefore Easdale you have to cross the Atlantic, but don't worry there is no need for passports, boats and ferries as you simply drive over the Atlantic Bridge and arrive at Tigh a Truish ('house of the trousers'). Locals travelling from the Isle of Seil to the mainland in the late eighteenth century would change here from their kilted plaids into trousers to avoid arrest (the wearing of kilted tartan had been banned by the Dress Act 1746 as part of the Act of Proscription, discussed more in treasures 72 and 76).

Continuing on along the single track road you will come to the village of Easdale; from there board the rib ferry boat to the Isle of Easdale. There is a small charge which is payable to the boatman, although be aware that the boat can be cancelled due to tide and weather conditions at a moment's notice. The crew will always try their best to get you over and back whatever the weather with the minimal amount of soaking. The journey over to the Isle of Easdale takes less than three minutes, which is part of what makes it so memorable.

The ferry arrives at the old mine workers village. The Isle of Easdale is a big lump of slate and the community existed there to mine the slate, making it a rather cool yet bizarre looking place. As you set off to explore around the island you'll first notice that there are wheelbarrows with numbers on them - the island's population, fifty-nine at the time of writing, use the barrows to get food from the boat to their homes. As you walk around the island, you will see steep-sided lagoons; this is where the mines were located and as they are no longer in use they have a certain eerie feel about them. When you find yourself on the more exposed ocean side of the island, there is a small stony beach which is covered in the best stones for stone skimming (skipping if you're North American). It is these stones along with the lagoons that have made the Isle of Easdale the location of the World Stone Skimming Championships. Yes you read that correctly.

People and competitors travel from all over the world to watch and compete in this event. If you'd like to see the 'arena', simply walk past the museum (it's signposted) and you will see a large lump of slate that is used as the stance for the competitors. Find a stone and have a go. Once you are back on the Isle of Seil again a visit to Easdale village is not complete without a visit to the tourist shop - an experience in itself. The staff are very friendly and welcome you into their Aladdin's cave of souvenirs. All in all it makes for a fun and fascinating day out.

How to get there:

The Isle of Seil is located south of Oban on Scotland's west coast. From the A816 turn onto the B844 and keep following signs to Easdale. From Easdale village you take the ferry to the Isle of Easdale.

30. Isle of Kerrera

What you'll discover:

The Isle of Kerrera protects Oban bay where the main ferry terminal serving the Inner and Outer Hebrides is located. The town of Oban is thus referred to as the 'Gateway to the Isles'. King Alexander II of Scotland died on the Isle of Kerrera on the sixth of July 1249, during his campaign to rid Scotland of Viking rule. He was taken to Melrose Abbey for burial (Iona had lost its status by this time) and the task fell to his son Alexander III, who brought the Lords of the Isles under his control (discussed in treasure number 18).

When visiting and exploring Kerrera my best advice is to hire a mountain bike in Oban and take it over on the short ferry journey, because you'll be able to cover the island more easily. If you are staying on the island you may find that decent walking boots are adequate. The island has a very peaceful feel and you'd be forgiven for thinking that you're absolutely miles away from civilisation. The Kerrera Tea Garden is worth stopping at for a rest and refreshment, and don't miss the detour down to Gylen Castle, a very impressively located ruin dating from the late sixteenth century which is free to visit.

As you explore keep an eye out for the seal colony, otters, wild goats and, if you're really lucky, the odd sea eagle. In the north of island you'll find the Hutcheson Memorial built in memory of David Hutcheson, who was the first to run a ferry service to the Western Isles in 1835. If time allows it's worth booking into the Waypoint Bar and Grill as it does some lovely seafood dishes amongst other food offerings, they even provide a boat service back to Oban from the restaurant. Time can just run away from you when exploring this beautiful wee island.

How to get there:

Take the road towards the ferry port in Oban and instead of turning into the terminal, keep going down Gallanach Road and within a few miles you come to the Kerrera ferry. No advanced booking is required; there is a small charge for the ferry which is paid to the operator.

31. Calgary Bay

What you'll discover:

The road from Tobermory to Calgary Bay on the Isle of Mull is not for the faint-hearted. There are literally dozens of bends, many of them hairpin and tight, plus you will have to be aware of other roads users and use the passing places provided.

There are not a huge amount of sandy beaches on Mull, which makes Calgary Bay even more special. The name means 'Beach of the Meadow', where the 'Cal' part from Gaelic means 'firm sand where a boat can be landed', and the 'gary' part means 'meadow'. The name suggests that there was a fishing community based here at one time, and this is confirmed nearby where there are remnants of an old clearance village (the clearances are discussed in treasure number 76). Beyond that there is the suggestion of an old fortification most likely from the Iron Age, so though there are not many people here now, there once was.

Calgary House, a short distance from the beach, was built in 1817. Although it is often referred to as Calgary Castle due to its castellated look, it was always a house. It is said that in the summer of 1876 Colonel James Macleod, who was Commissioner of the North-West Mounted Police (Mounties) in Canada, visited Calgary House and shortly after returning to Canada, he suggested its name for Fort Calgary. This in turn became the modern city of Calgary in the province of Alberta. Interestingly the actor David Tennant of Dr Who fame traced his ancestry to Calgary Bay.

I first visited Calgary Bay when I was sixteen with my family, on our way to Dervaig to go on a whale watching trip which was amazing - we spotted lots of Humpbacks and a calf came right up and circled our boat twice. A year later as a daft seventeen year old I returned with my friends and we decided to rough camp next to the burn that flows into the bay. It was a beautiful sunny day with an amazing sunset, although I was struggling to fully enjoy the spectacle due to being very badly sunburnt...got to love those happy memories of the innocence of youth! Helen and I visited in 2012 and enjoyed a nice romantic walk along the sands followed by a picnic as the sun was setting - I managed to enjoy the second sunset much more than the first. Calgary Bay is a truly beautiful place.

How to get there:

Calgary Bay is located twelve miles west of Tobermory on the B8073. Check your brakes and have your wits about you before driving this road.

32. Isle of Staffa

What you'll discover:

If you are visiting the Isle of Iona then the Isle of Staffa, located a short distance to the north, is an absolute must. Staffa is a small rocky outcrop entirely made from volcanic basalt. The name is Norse in origin meaning 'stave' or 'pillar' and this is due to the basalt pillars of rock that meet you as you arrive. Think of Staffa as part of the Scottish end of the Giant's Causeway, which is found over on the other side of the North Channel in Northern Ireland.

The Isle of Staffa became more popular and known about in the Victorian era; indeed it was actually visited by Queen Victoria herself. Another famous visitor was Felix Mendelssohn; after his visit in 1829 he was inspired to write his 'Hebrides Overture' having been inside the large, almost cathedral-like Fingal's Cave on the Island. I decided to give a rendition of 'Flower of Scotland' to test the acoustics of the cave and decided they certainly enhanced my otherwise poor attempt to sing.

When Helen and I visited in the month of October, we discovered small white seal pups in the various coves. We wandered down to get a closer look, although we didn't get too close because disturbing pups can lead to their mothers abandoning them. It was amazing to see these wonderful animals from a distance but we decided to leave nature well alone and carry on our exploring. If Staffa doesn't move you in even the smallest of ways then nothing will.

How to get there:

Travel to Fionnphort on the Isle of Mull and then chose a boat operator for the trip to the Isles of Staffa and Iona - there are a couple of operators available offering a similar service. Boat trips are weather dependant so calling ahead would be recommended.

33. The Golden Road

What you'll discover:

Harris and Lewis in the Outer Hebrides is one land mass, but they are referred to as separate islands. They are very different and in fact Harris itself is an island of complete contrast. On the western Atlantic side of the island, you drive past amazingly clear and empty golden beaches (as described in treasure number 34). Near the beaches you can see the remnants of an old agricultural way of farming which involved the creation of ridged strips of land referred to as 'lazy beds' on the Western Isles. In much of the rest of Scotland they were simply called 'rigs' which is Scots for ridge. The grass is green and the land has a soft textural feel to it with grey rocky outcrops.

Travel to the eastern Minch (the name of the seaway between the Western Isles/Inner Hebrides and the mainland of Scotland) side of the island and it is an entirely different story. This is where you find the 'Golden Road'. The name is interesting and there seems to be some ambiguity as to why it is referred to as this. Some say the name relates to the cost of building it, others say that its creation saved lives because previously people had been washed away in swollen rivers, and some say that the main surveyor for the roads construction, a Mr A. S. Matheson, looked upon its building as his best and most memorable work. Whatever the reason it's an awesome road to drive. It takes you through some of the best scenery to be found on the Western Isles. It is a rugged and raw landscape; the grey rock that you see all around you is Lewisian Gneiss (the name originating from the neighbouring island), the oldest rock type to be found in the British Isles, and amongst the oldest rock types in the world at over three billion years old.

It is a barren, inhospitable, yet beautiful place, interspersed with wee lochans, some of which have lilies in them. Beauty is said to be in the eye of the beholder - I remember someone said to me that they didn't like it because it was 'too harsh'. It is because of this stark rawness that it was used in Stanley Kubrick's 1968 Sci-Fi film '2001; A Space Odyssey', to create a perceived lunar landscape.

As you drive the Golden Road, stop regularly to take it in and remember that the rock surrounding you is mind-bogglingly old.

How to get there:

If travelling from Lewis on the A859, once past Tarbert you'll see the sign to the left. If you have just arrived at Leverburgh then as you leave the ferry terminus turn right and travel the short distance on the A859 towards Rodel - thereafter you are starting on the Golden Road.

34. Luskentyre and Hushinish beaches

What you'll discover:

The west coast of Harris has some of the most amazing beaches not only to be found in Scotland but arguably in the world. Although the beach at Luskentyre is easily accessible from the main road, the fact that the Outer Hebrides is one of the most sparsely populated areas in Europe, and not overrun with visitors means that you'll easily find a quiet place to enjoy this pristine beach. You may be tempted to take a dip in the aquamarine water - be warned it's 'fresh' to say the least - although once you're in and used to it you'll be fine. Helen and I went swimming here in 2013; it was an amazing sunny day and such a serene place to be. We could have easily been fooled into thinking we were in Thailand...had the ambient temperature been at least twenty degrees centigrade higher. Funnily enough, in 2009 a beautiful beach photo from Berneray (not far to the south of Harris) was mistakenly used in promotional material by the Thai Tourism Board to promote Kai Bae beach in Thailand. I'd imagine whoever was responsible would have been ever so slightly embarrassed to find out that the beach they used was in the far north west of Scotland!

If you seek complete seclusion then head to the west of Harris and you'll find Hushinish beach. Although smaller than Luskentyre, Hushinish beach is well worth the extra effort. On the way you'll pass the surprising and rather grand Amhuinnsuidhe (pronounced 'Avenshee') Castle/House which dates back to 1865. I was told that the name means the 'seat next to the river', however the spelling is interesting as the first part of the name certainly means river, however the 'suidhe' part (pronounced 'shee' - discussed in treasure number

37) sounds like a reference to the faerie folk so maybe the name actually means the 'faerie river'. Give yourself plenty of time to travel to both Luskentyre and Hushinish beaches and time to stop and relax once there.

How to get there:

Luskentyre beach is around ten miles from Tarbert - follow the main A859 then take signs for the beach. For Hushinish follow the B887, a single track road, for approximately fourteen miles until you get to the end.

35. The Butt of Lewis

What you'll discover:

The Butt of Lewis is part of an area referred to as Ness, meaning peninsula, at the most northerly point of the Isle of Lewis. You can stand next to the lighthouse, built in the 1860s and different from most Scottish lighthouses because it is built of brick and remains unpainted, and when you look out into the North Atlantic it feels like you are on the edge of the world. That's certainly how the Romans felt about the north west of Scotland when they sailed around and mapped the coast, referring to it as the ends of the earth. For a landlubber like me I certainly got a real sense of foreboding whilst standing looking off into the dark blue yonder.

That said every year in autumn a small group of ten hardy local men (referred to as the Men of Ness) sail to a rocky outcrop forty miles north of the Ness called Sula Sgeir. They hunt and catch seabirds, but not just any seabird, their targets are young gannets called guga. The name Sula Sgeir means the 'gannet rock' from Old Norse and this is a tradition that has lasted dozens of generations. Many people today object to this annual hunt as they see it as unnecessary and inhumane, but the participating locals say it is an ancient tradition, that it is sustainable and conducted in a humane manner. It is a tricky subject matter, but currently the annual hunt still takes place on a very limited licence. Disputes aside, you can imagine the ancient people of the land conducting this type of annual event as it was absolutely essential to help them survive in this tough and exposed place. Prior to visiting this area of Lewis I recommend reading a crime thriller called The Blackhouse by Peter May, where the local area and the tradition of the guga hunt are brought to life in his writing.

How to get there:

Travel north on the A857 to the Port of Ness, then take a left onto the small single track road to the lighthouse.

36. Isles of Barra and Vatersay

What you'll discover:

Barra is the most southerly inhabited island in the Outer Hebrides, and the most westerly inhabited Island in Scotland. It has a very strong sense of community, tradition, and heritage for which it has won awards. Getting to the Isle of Barra does require a bit of effort - you can either travel by ferry directly from Oban, which can be a rough five hour ride across the Minch as experienced by Helen and myself in a force eight gale (although it wasn't *that* bad according to a local we got speaking to), or you can arrive from Eriskay, south of the Uists, by the small but scenic car ferry. Alternatively you can arrive by plane...yes that's right Barra, with its population of less than two thousand, has its very own airport, and also has the only aeroplane timetable in the world which is governed by the movement of the tides. You land at Traigh Mhor ('big beach') where it is possible to go cockling although you have to avoid the 'runway'.

The island has a wealth of history and heritage and it's just wonderful to explore. Barra's climate is like much of the Western Isles in that it rarely sees snow, frost is quite unusual, and average annual temperatures don't vary that wildly but daylight hours do. A visit to Kisimul Castle, former seat of Clan MacNeil, is worth considering; it sits on its rocky outcrop a few hundred metres off the shore at Castlebay, the 'capital' of Barra.

To the south of Barra, linked by a causeway, is the small island of Vatersay, with its beautiful white sandy beaches. Vatersay beach is one of the more secluded to be found, and offers protection from the wind which generally blows from a south westerly direction. The beach itself has lovely views looking north over Castlebay, and is a real treasure.

How to get there:

The A888 is the main road that circles around Barra, with its attractions signposted. The Isle of Vatersay lies to the south of Castlebay.

37. Faerie Glen

What you'll discover:

I first visited the Faerie Glen in March 2002 and as I drove in the first thought that crossed my mind was 'Hobbiton'! Locally it is called Balnaknock which means 'the village of hills'. In the middle of the cluster of small conical hills or faerie knolls, there is a rocky outcrop which resembles the type of rock that castles such as Edinburgh or Stirling sit upon, and is referred to as the faerie castle. The locals who live in the glen call the outcrop 'Caisteal an Eoghainn', meaning Ewan's Castle. Ewan was a local shepherd from a bygone era; apparently he used to stand at the top of the outcrop to command his dogs.

Everything in the glen is small; from the wiry, twisted hazel trees to the wee lochan called 'Lochan Morag Dearg', meaning Red Morag's Lochan. Morag was a lady who lived in an old blackhouse next to lochan, and if you look carefully you can still see remnants of her small rectangular house today.

There was a time when the belief in faerie folklore was very strong right across Scotland. It was understood that the faerie folk were not to be messed or meddled with. When you talk about faerie folklore today people will generally smirk and say it's childlike or just superstitious nonsense. There is a tendency to think of images of Tinkerbell and wee fluttery creatures that live in the rhubarb patch at the bottom of the garden. This benevolent image of faeries was developed in the eighteenth and nineteenth centuries, and is not the faerie folklore of old that the ancient people knew and understood.

The 'wee folk', 'the guid folk', or in the Gaelic language the 'sidhe' or 'sith' (pronounced shee), were/are smallish beings with many human physical attributes. They exist in a world 'in-between'; a sort of other dimension somewhere between dreams and reality, between our world and the underworld, or both! I was lucky once to get chatting to a local who lived at the end of the glen and who was very well versed in the lore of the faerie folk. He took time to speak with me at length, passing on knowledge that gave me a far greater understanding of the folklore and its meaning, but also how best to keep the wee folk on your side. He told me that they love music and having fun but can change their mood in a moment; they don't like iron, swearing, or you putting your hands in your pockets; they also don't like things being taken from the glen (or any of their places for that matter). They can be very giving and generous, but sinister and mischievous in equal measure. You should never accept a gift from a faerie - it may appear to be something amazing but there will be downside rest assured. To protect yourself, property and children, you should plant the Rowan tree (also known as Mountain Ash). The gentleman I spoke with had nine Rowan trees growing around his property, and he freely admitted that he and his family were in no doubt that the wee folk existed so were taking no chances.

I have been fortunate enough to have visited the glen hundreds of times and I still love going back. I'll admit that some odd things have happened over the years, things that certainly made me stop in my tracks. On one occasion, I picked up some rubbish that had been left and heard a shout of "get out of here!" When I looked up there was nobody in the vicinity, only an angry looking crow which then swooped towards me. I left feeling somewhat perturbed by the incident.

Interestingly, I have always been lucky with the weather when I've returned since, even on miserable, dreich (grey and drizzly) days the weather has lifted whilst I've been there. On that basis I think I'm on reasonably good terms with the wee folk of the glen...long may that remain the case.

Today the Faerie Glen is much more known about than it was back in 2002 thanks to the internet, and although it is a bit busy for me it still retains that special feeling. Please visit and enjoy, but keep these words of warning in mind (said to me by the local man) - "Son, you're very welcome here as long as you respect the place" - wise words indeed.

How to get there:

On the main A87 between Portree and Uig there is a turning for Balnaknock on the outskirts of Uig village. Travel along this single track road for approximately one and a half miles until you see the lochan and faerie knolls. Park sensibly as locals require access.

38. Loch Coruisk boat trip

What you'll discover:

Loch Coruisk, or 'lake of the cauldron of waters', sounds very impressive and does not disappoint - when it comes to boat trips this has to be on the list of treasures. The whole experience starts when you leave from Elgol and travel into and past Camasunary Bay. It really is like travelling into another world. The Black Cuillin Mountains, with their dark gabbro rock, thrust up from the water and rise into towering pinnacles above, giving the place such an imposing feel.

The first time I saw this landscape it made me think of images that would be conjured up by reading Tolkien's Lord of the Rings. The Isle of Skye and the Cuillin Mountains are unique in Scotland; there really is nothing else quite like them to be found in this country. They are volcanic in origin and what you see today was once the inside of an ancient, long-extinct, super volcano, with the exterior layers of rock long since worn away by ancient glaciations.

As the scenery opens out into Loch Coruisk it is simply breathtaking and I don't use that word often. The water of the loch is dark and mysterious, and is supposed to have a resident Kelpie (see treasure number 66). The boat is the easiest way in to Loch Coruisk - you can walk from Elgol however it does involve negotiating a tricky cliff called the 'bad step', or you can walk down Glen Sligachan from the north but be properly prepared if that is your preferred way of getting there. Whichever way you choose you'll love it.

Helen and I travelled there the day after we got engaged on the Isle of Raasay (treasure number 39), and the staff on the Bella Jane gave us some fizz to say congratulations which was very kind and thoughtful of them. The splendour of Loch Coruisk reminds me of a conversation I had once with an old gentleman in the village of Kyleakin (he was a retired fisherman so I use the term 'gentlemen' loosely). He said "the Isle of Skye is the jewel in the Scottish crown when it comes to scenery". I replied in agreement, although now I think I'd alter his comment by saying that the Isle of Skye is one of the more spectacular of the *many* jewels in the Scottish crown when it comes to scenery.

How to get there:

Travel to Broadford and take the B8083 to Elgol. It is recommended you book the boat trip to Loch Coruisk in advance, and contact your operator before making the journey to Elgol because the weather and sea conditions are variable.

39. Isle of Raasay

What you'll discover:

Skye is amazing of course and dwarfs the Isle of Raasay in every physical way, but because you have to take a ferry to Raasay (unlike Skye where there is the option of a land bridge), it is much quieter as a result, and retains a very special feeling.

There are a number of reasons that Helen and I hold this island very close to our hearts. Firstly, it was the clan home of the MacSween's who happen to make our favourite brands of haggis. Secondly, we both love the story of a local man called Calum MacLeod. Calum built one and three quarter miles of road by hand using nothing more than a pickaxe, a shovel, a few sticks of 'borrowed' dynamite, a wheelbarrow, and a whole lot of guts and determination. There is a book that covers this story called 'Calum's Road' which is worth a read. The local council had refused to build a road between Brochel Castle (worth stopping at for a look) and Arnish, where Calum and his wife lived. Calum believed that without a reasonable road to Arnish the community that he had lived in for almost all his life would not survive. Greater access was necessary to allow people to move around more freely. Over the span of ten years beginning in 1964, Calum doggedly carved out his road. Years later, after Calum had sadly passed away in 1988, his road was adopted by the council and a proper tarmac finish was applied. Although Calum did not live to see it, thankfully the community that he dearly loved survived, and now it has grown in number thanks to his hard work and perseverance. Taking a drive, cycle or walk along it is quite a bizarre experience and slightly hair-raising in places but a must do.

The third, final and main reason that Helen and I love Raasay so much is because it was on top of the highest hill on the island - the extinct volcano of Dun Caan - that we got engaged in October 2015. We were so lucky as the weather was clear and fine, the walk was far enough without being too much of a stretch, and the views from the top were absolutely amazing. Make time for Raasay and you will be greatly rewarded.

How to get there:

As you travel on the A87 between Broadford and Portree on the Isle of Skye, you will come to the small settlement of Sconser - from here you take the Calmac ferry over to the Island and return the same way.

40. Loch Shianta

What you'll discover:

There is much on the internet about visiting the Faerie Pools in Glen Brittle on the Isle of Skye. They are stunning, of that there is no doubt, and I have swam there many times - even in February, which looking back was a bit foolhardy but I proved my masculinity to a bunch of Australians I was with...I think. When I first started going to the Faerie Pools there was barely a track to take you there and no proper parking. They were, and still are, one of the most charming places that I have ever been to, not only in Scotland but the world. However, nothing ever stands still; Skye is a busier place than ever, and today there is now a proper track and car park, and thus many more visitors who are now very aware of this place thanks to Tripadvisor and books on wild swimming. So if you are going to Skye please do visit the Faerie Pools, but just be aware that the charm is not quite as strong as it once was.

That said it is still possible to find alternative pristine, aquamarine and enchanting pools on Skye and one of these is Loch Shianta. The name derives from Gaelic and could have several meanings such as the 'small loch of the faeries', 'the loch of the faerie hill' or possibly the 'peaceful lochan'. The first two are more likely given the name starting with 'shi' (shee). It is viewed as a sacred, healing and holy lochan on Skye, and thankfully due to its location there is very limited parking so the number of people able to get down at any one time will always be restricted.

Walk down the small track, and when you reach Loch Shianta it is also worth exploring through the bushes and trees on the far side where you can see the crystal clear water flowing into the lochan from four small burns. The water is beautifully clear and has a real aquamarine colour due to the light sand at the bottom. If the weather is fair you may wish to go for a wee swim; if not maybe just dip your face - or your feet - in.

How to get there:

Loch Shianta is located near Flodigarry on Skye's Trotternish peninsula. There is a small information board in the parking area. Walk all the way down the path to the loch.

41. Kylerhea - Glenelg Ferry and Brochs

What you'll discover:

How many places can you visit in the world that are not only palindromic but are also twinned with their namesake on another planet? Not many I suspect but Glenelg is one of them - although to be clear, this treasure is Glenelg in the Highlands, not Glenelg on Mars.

Whether you are travelling to or leaving from the Isle of Skye, it is well worth the detour to take the Kylerhea – Glenelg ferry and visit the brochs located nearby. Originally built in 1969, MV Glenachulish was first used as the car ferry at Ballachulish near Glencoe. In 1975 the Ballachulish Bridge opened and the ferry relocated to Glenelg. The vessel is the last manually operated turntable ferry in the world, and still owned and operated by friendly staff, making it a very a unique experience. On previous visits I've spotted sea eagles, otters playing by the shore, seals popping their heads up for a look and - the icing on the cake - a small pod of whales.

On the mainland at Glenelg, there a number of historical sites of note but my personal favourites are the Brochs of Dun Troddan and Dun Telve. Brochs are uniquely Scottish; they were primarily defensive structures but would also have served as very obvious symbols of status and power dating back two thousand years to the Iron Age. In total there are at least five hundred in Scotland, with the vast majority located in the north and west of the country, generally near the coast. Although there are traces of brochs found elsewhere, their presence is less well documented. They are very cleverly designed involving two circular concentric dry stone walls (or as we would say it in Scotland dry stane dykes), with interconnecting slabs of stone used to stabilise the two structures. From a distance brochs slightly resemble the shape of cooling towers found at modern power stations. There is no mortar used to bind the structure together, relying instead on the cumulative compressive pressure of the interlocking stones. In the void between the inner and outer rings there were stairways constructed to give easy access to the upper levels. There were no windows, only one entrance at ground level, and the lowest level seems to have been used for storing animals whilst the upper levels were for human accommodation.

Why were brochs built? Many historians say the main threats were from rival neighbouring tribes or families looking to take livestock and possessions, and brochs were primarily a defensive structure. However, more recent theories point to an external threat in the form of the Romans. In the early part of the first century CE the Romans were trying to conquer the whole of Britannia. Brochs would have made excellent temporary hideaway structures that could protect people and their livestock for long enough for a threat to pass. In time brochs were adopted as more permanent homes, generally by the most prominent family within the local area.

Although the best preserved broch today is Mousa on the Shetland Isles, the two found in Glenelg are very fine examples.

How to get there:

Glenelg is located a short distance from the A87 at Glen Shiel - follow signs for the Kylerhea ferry. If travelling from the Isle of Skye, take the Kylerhea road from just south of Breakish. The ferry operates in the summer only and it is worth calling ahead to check sailings.

42. Achmelvich beach and Lochinver Larder

What you'll discover:

If it is peace, tranquillity, and seclusion that you seek, you will find them all and more at Achmelvich beach. The name in English is a bit of a giveaway as it means the 'meadow by the sandy dunes' - I'd argue it is a lot more impressive than the name suggests but still a fitting description nonetheless. Achmelvich is a wee white sandy beach located at the end of a single track road in the north west Highlands. With a bit of exploring there are other smaller beaches nearby, however it's the whole surroundings that make this place a wee piece of paradise.

Achmelvich beach lies only three miles from the village of Lochinver, but don't let the short distance lure you into thinking it's an easy drive - they are three very long miles, although well worth the effort. When Helen and I were here in 2014 we were blessed with an amazing spell of sunshine...only to be followed by sudden rain...to then be followed by sunshine again. We also saw a very impressive stag pop his head up from the nearby rocks which was a real treat.

Before going to the beach you must stock up on your picnic - nothing beats a good pie and the ones you buy in Lochinver Larder are delicious. Of all the pies I have ever eaten in my life (believe me there have been quite a few), the pies from Lochinver Larder beat every other contender by a good country mile (appropriate usage of the term given the journey to the beach). It is not just the quality of the pies but also the variety - you can choose from a great selection of meat and vegetarian options. We couldn't decide so bought far more than we required and ended up eating them for days after our visit. Oh the hardship! Or as we'd say in the Scots tongue it was a 'sair fecht'!

The peace and the pies make Achmelvich and Lochinver a must do.

How to get there:

Lochinver is located at the end of the A837. To travel to the beach, head out of the village and turn onto B869. Take care on this interesting road.

43. Smoo Cave

What you'll discover:

I said in my introduction that Scotland doesn't always have the largest of everything. But when it comes to the largest sea cave in Britain, it has this in the form of Smoo Cave. It measures two hundred feet deep, one hundred and thirty feet wide and fifty feet high. Although it is called Smoo Cave singular, there are in fact three caves that are accessible, the innermost by a small boat. The formation of the caves is interesting as the outer sea cave was created by erosion from tidal waves (although today the sea rarely makes it into the cave as the land has risen after the last Ice Age), but the interior caves were created by freshwater from the Smoo burn.

The name often causes a bit of bemusement but it is said to have derived from 'smjugg' or 'smuga' in Old Norse (like so many place names in the north and west of Scotland), and either means a hole/cleft or a hiding place. Therefore it will be of no surprise that this place has a few legends and stories. It was a place of refuge and counter attack when the local Mackay clan were attacked unexpectedly by the Gunns. The Mackays ran into the cave and hid. When the pursuing Gunn clansmen reached the cave, they were set upon and none survived.

The cave was also used for the illicit distilling of the Uisge Beatha (meaning 'water of life', pronounced 'ooshka bae' then corrupted into the word whisky). However after the 1746 Act of Proscription came into force on the first of August banning the distilling of whisky (amongst other things), production was moved elsewhere, the cave considered to be too obvious. Apparently the ghosts of two excisemen - who 'accidentally' drowned under the waterfall inside the cave after heavy rain - still haunt the caves to this day.

Despite the alleged ghosts, the caves are a great place to visit. The path from the road gives you access to the outer cave. If the weather is kind and the burn not too full you can take the wee boat trip into the interior cave.

How to get there:

The cave(s) are located just off and literally under the A838 about a mile and half east of Durness on the north coast of Sutherland. There is a car park with toilets, from there just carefully follow the track down.

Food and Drink

Scotland produces some of the best food and drink in the world. From humble cuisine such as haggis or oatcakes to seafood that provides the most prestigious fine-dining restaurants with their catch of the day. Of course no meal would be complete without some very fine beverages to wash it all down with, and Scotland produces a plethora of these. Slàinte mhath!

44. Cromars Fish and Chip Shop

What you'll discover:

Although relatively new on the 'chippy' (slang for chip shop) scene being established in 2013, Cromars has stormed into the premier league of chippies and has won Scotland's Best Fish and Chip Shop in 2016 and 2017. Centrally located in St. Andrews town centre, Cromars is easily found. You will find the usual chip shop offerings but Cromars also serves up some quality cuisine such as mussels and scallops. The staff are friendly, and a nice touch is that you can find out the name of the boat that landed the fish, and who supplied the potatoes for the chips. The tartare sauce is homemade and tastes amazing. You can sit in or take away - my preference is to take away and find a quiet bench to sit and watch the world go by.

Visitors travel from all over the world to St. Andrews for many different reasons, not just for fish and chips. For some it is the draw of the game of golf - St. Andrews is referred to as the 'home of golf' - people come to play the famous courses and visit the recently renovated British Golf Museum. For others it is the history of St. Andrews that attracts them; intriguing history lurks around every corner wherever you go in the town. You can visit the ruins of what was at one time Scotland's greatest Cathedral, and take the opportunity to climb St Rule's Tower with amazing three hundred and sixty three degree views from the top (well worth the effort on a clear day). The University is the oldest in Scotland at over six hundred years old and attracts students from across the globe as well as royalty. St. Andrews is where the sixteenth century reformation of the Scottish church began, with John Knox preaching a new form of Christianity called Calvinism (adopted as the official religion in 1560).

The wide open West Sands beach, adjacent to St. Andrews Old Course, is where the famous 1983 'Chariots of Fire' scene was filmed, and where in 2010 another much less famous race took place. I was soundly beaten by Helen in a sprint with shouts from bystanders of "gan yersel big man!" I put my loss down to the fact I was wearing hiking boots and carrying quite a bit more weight than my opponent but of course I was kidding myself...I was beaten fair and square, and the dent to my ego has taken years to come to terms with.

With so much to see and do you will need quality sustenance and what better than fish and chips, especially on the coast, and where better than the best in Scotland 2016/2017.

How to get there:

Cromars is located at the junction of Market Street and Union Street in St. Andrews old town.

45. Arbroath Smokies and Forfar Bridies

What you'll discover:

This treasure covers a delicious foodie duo and a declaration of intent. Food first: within the European Union certain food and drink come under the select status of the EU Protected Food Name Scheme. Arbroath Smokies are in this elite group, along with Stornoway black pudding, Orkney beef, Scotch whisky and many more.

Essentially a 'smokie' is oak smoked haddock but it is done in a way particular to Arbroath. Some say that smokies originated 3 miles north in Auchmithie when a barn storing barrels of salted haddock caught fire and burned down. Some of the fish got smoked inside the charred barrels and on opening these barrels the locals discovered a great new flavour to their daily catch. This seems an odd tale given that for centuries fish was preserved by smoking it, but as all tour guides will tell you, you should never let the truth get in the way of a good story. The best way to eat a smokie is heated with a bit of melted butter. They are also delicious in fish pies.

Whilst in Arbroath it would be remiss of you not to visit the Abbey. It was here in 1320 where Robert the Bruce, with his clergy and noblemen, wrote a very eloquent letter to the Pope requesting that he reaffirm Scottish sovereignty and tell Edward II of England to give up his claim to the Scottish throne. It took another eight years and a change of Pope and English King for this to happen, proving that patience is a virtue.

The second foodie delight is the Forfar Bridie. Many people will have tried some kind of meat pastry at some point in their lives, and for those who enjoy a good pie/pastry, the sampling of this meaty delight should be on their list. On a daily basis right across Scotland, bakers will make meat or onion (handy for vegetarians) bridies - the vast majority of which will be made using puff pastry. And here lies the difference - a Forfar Bridie uses a shortcrust pastry! This may sound like a minor detail but it does make a real difference to the textural experience, and shortcrust pastry is far less messy. There are two providers in the centre of Forfar - McLaren Baker's and William Saddlers and Sons - both offer high quality bridies.

How to get there:

Arbroath is located on the A92 on Scotland's east coast. Forfar is inland and is a relatively short drive from Arbroath on a cross country route. Worth it for the bridies though!

46. Loch Fyne Oyster Bar and Fyne Ales

What you'll discover:

The west of Scotland is blessed with the Gulf Stream. If we did not have its warming influence, Scotland would have a climate more akin to Alaska than the cool temperate climate that we have today. The fjordlike inlets and sea lochs found right up the west coast of Scotland are havens for a vast array of marine habitat, particularly shellfish, and it is on the west coast we find these treasures.

On the way to Loch Fyne from Loch Lomond, you'll cross over the highest point on the A83 known as the 'Rest and be Thankful', which originally refers to a stone plaque put there by the soldiers who built the original road back in 1753. On arrival travellers could rest and be thankful that they had reached the highest point and whichever way they were going thereafter it would be mostly a downhill journey. It's worth stopping on a fair day to enjoy the views down Glen Croe.

The fine dining restaurant and delicatessen on Loch Fyne that you see today is the result of a lot of hard work and the pursuit of excellence, with a keen eye on the environment and sustainability. Their seafood journey began back in 1978 when a local landowner and a marine biologist put their heads together to create the Loch Fyne Oyster Bar. Originally selling oysters from a shed next to the road, in time came many awards for quality and of course with the accolades came further demand. Through clever and sustainable aquaculture Loch Fyne seafood has now diversified into a chain of restaurants, and their products are exported globally.

You can eat in the restaurant, or do what Helen and I prefer to do which is to buy the great produce from the deli and take it away to a scenic spot of our choosing for a picnic. Of course no picnic is complete without a fine (no pun intended) beverage to accompany it. The best libation is provided just a few miles away up Glen Fyne in the form of the Fyne Ales Brewery. Established in 2000, this micro-brewery has won many awards for its quality and innovative beer offerings. Take a tour or simply sample the ale, and you'll be well on your way to taste heaven. Happy days!

How to get there:

Loch Fyne Oyster Bar and Fyne Ales Brewery are both located off the A83 near the scenic town of Inveraray. Both are well signposted.

47. Abhainn Dearg Distillery

What you'll discover:

This is the only whisky distillery in this book. Although there are numerous taste and visitor experiences to be had with whisky, they are all different and unique to an individual. There are also many guidebooks on whisky, written by experts who are far better versed than I. Don't get me wrong, I like whisky and know a fair bit about it, but not enough to write about it. However as an experience, Helen and I enjoyed visiting the Abhainn Dearg (pronounced 'aveen jerrig', meaning 'red river') distillery for a number of reasons. Because it is a relatively new distillery and done on a small scale, you get a more rustic, and dare I say raw, experience. There are no staff in shirts and ties chatting to you from a script written by someone in an office, and there's no shiny high tech visitor centre. There is just something more natural about the overall experience, maybe this is due to the size and location of the distillery in the remote west of the Isle of Lewis. You certainly get more of the personal touch than you would visiting a larger more commercial distillery.

We were lucky enough to be taken around the distillery (the shed) by the owner and distiller Mark (Marko) Tayburn himself - his passion made for a very real experience that many other distilleries lack. To be completely honest the whisky didn't particularly suit my taste, but was still perfectly drinkable. On these occasions when I taste new whiskies that I find aren't for me, I am always reminded of the best advice I was given regarding whisky. I once asked a very experienced whisky drinker "what is the best whisky?'". He pondered the question for a moment and then responded by saying "finding the perfect whisky for you is like finding your perfect partner in life. It takes time and experience but you'll find both eventually". How right he was - I have found the partner, just not the whisky...yet.

When Helen and I visited in 2013, the tours were free so to show my appreciation I bought a bottle of the Spirit of Lewis. We loved the sense of something honest and real, with a proper enthusiastic person behind it. Today the tours currently cost £5 per person, but it is worth paying for something more authentic.

Near to the distillery you can visit Uig beach which is famous for the discovery of a very rare set of medieval chess pieces, made from walrus ivory and whale teeth, dating from the twelfth century and known as the Lewis Chessmen. Folklore says that the man who discovered them in 1831 thought they were a box of faeries and ran away, only to return later with some help to retrieve them. Perhaps the poor fellow had been imbibing too much whisky himself that day.

When raising a toast with your newly purchased whisky say the words 'slàinte mhath' (pronounced slonsha va) meaning 'good health'!

How to get there:

The distillery is located on the B8011 near Uig on the Isle of Lewis, approximately an hour's drive from the island's capital, Stornoway.

Walks

Thanks to Scotland's varied terrain there will be a walk for you, no matter what your ability is - whether it's scrambling up a mountainside or a mellower riverside stroll, you'll find walking options in abundance. Appropriate footwear is required for each of these walks, and I'd recommend the excellent Walkhighlands website for detailed route information.

48. Eildon Hills and Trimontium

What you'll discover:

This walk begins and ends at Melrose Abbey. It takes in amazing three hundred and sixty degree views across the rolling Borders landscape and the Tweed basin, local faerie folklore, the location of the most important Roman fort ever built in Scotland, and a village that could be the oldest and longest continuously inhabited in Scotland.

Start at the very impressive Cistercian Abbey of Melrose, one of the best preserved pieces of gothic architecture in Scotland. Follow signs for the St Cuthbert's Way, a sixty two mile trail that goes from Melrose to Lindisfarne. The route will take you under the bypass and uphill out of the town - be sure not to miss the left hand turn to the Eildons, which takes you down an alleyway between two houses. Simply follow the track which takes you to the saddle between Eildon Hill North and Eildon Mid Hill. The third peak, Eildon Wester Hill, lies just to the south. It is well worth climbing all three Eildons, if time and ability allows.

From the summit of Eildon Hill North there is a grassy path that descends east to a disused road, known locally as the Bogle Burn road. Turn right and you will find an information board which tells the mysterious story of a local man by the name of Thomas of Learmont or Thomas of Ercildoune. He was lured by the beauty of the Faerie Queen, and after falling under her spell, was taken away into the realm of the wee folk, where it is said he stayed for three to seven years (depending on the source you read). On his return, Thomas was given the gift of prophecy but also could no longer tell a lie. All his prophecies were written in poetic rhymes, earning him the title 'Thomas the Rhymer'.

Between the information board and the Rhymer's Stone, there is a path that takes you down into the village of Newstead, where a right turn will take you along to where the largest Roman fort in Scotland - Trimontium (the Fort of the Three Hills) - was located. Unfortunately there is very little to be seen today of this once great fort, but there are information boards to help. Fascinatingly, archaeologists discovered the site of a basic amphitheatre, which would make it the most northerly located amphitheatre in the world.

From Trimontium, make your way back through Newstead, which claims to be the oldest village in Scotland due to it being established in Roman times. It has been continuously inhabited thereafter. The walk back to Melrose is either by road or via a small track past some stables, now following signs for the Borders Abbeys Way, another walking trail. Once back in Melrose you'll need some sustenance and there are plenty of choices, however Martin Baird the Butchers (located in the Square) does amazing steak slices and filling macaroni pies.

How to get there:

The town of Melrose located a short distance from the main A68 road. There is on street parking available. Melrose Abbey is centrally located and worth visiting.

49. Roslin Glen and Castle

What you'll discover:

Mention the name Roslin and people generally think of Rosslyn Chapel. The chapel is a beautiful and fascinating place and is well worth a visit, however following the publication of Dan Brown's book 'The Da Vinci Code', and the subsequent film starring Tom Hanks, visitor numbers have increased significantly. There is a new visitor centre and cafe as a result.

As interesting as the chapel is, it is the glen below that provides our treasure. Beyond the chapel lies a small cemetery, from where the path branches left to Roslin Castle. The name originates from the nearby River Esk - a 'ross' is a promontory or outcrop of rock or land, on which the castle was built on, and a 'linn' is a waterway or rapids, which the castle sits above. Hence Ross-Linn; then corrupted over the years into both Roslin and Rosslyn.

As the track goes deeper into the woods, you will find the ruins of the castle. Most of what remains dates from the thirteenth and fourteenth centuries, and there is one section still in use today providing holiday accommodation. The path continues down and around the castle rock, to the river below. Keep the river on your right as you explore the gorge and surrounding woods of Roslin Glen.

The glen is a place of real tranquillity; it is therefore astonishing to think that just a short distance away, one of the bloodiest medieval battles ever fought during the Scottish Wars of Independence occurred, on the twenty-fourth of February 1303. The Battle of Roslin Glen was a Scottish victory but at a huge loss of life. Some sources suggest that a total of over thirty five thousand men were killed - seven thousand Scots and a staggering twenty eight thousand English. Even if these numbers have been inflated over the years, there were still significant losses and yet this battle is rarely discussed unlike others of the time.

Despite this bloody chapter in its history, there is a special, reviving energy about Roslin Glen, and it is well worth taking the time to enjoy the abundance of nature that surrounds you.

How to get there:

The village of Roslin is located a short distance south of Edinburgh, on the B7006. Rosslyn Chapel is well signposted. If intending to visit the chapel, it is possible to park in their car park. Alternatively, there is ample on street parking in the village.

50. Goat Fell

What you'll discover:

The Isle of Arran is often described as 'Scotland in miniature'. This label comes from the fact that like mainland Scotland, the highest hills are found in the north and the lower fertile farmlands are found in the south. At eight hundred and seventy-four metres, Goat Fell is the highest mountain on the island. Scotland has nearly three hundred mountains of three thousand feet or more, classified as Munros. Although Goat Fell falls just short of this category, the walk starts almost at sea level, and ascends a height greater than many mainland Munros. It is thus more challenging than many expect.

The name 'Goat Fell' derives from Norse, again showing the Viking influence found in many locations and place names on Scotland's west coast.

The easiest place to start the walk is the Isle of Arran Brewery because there is a decent sized car park. There is a well established path that takes you through woodland, before emerging into a more exposed boulder field. Follow the well-trodden path to the summit, taking care in the upper sections where the rocks can be slippy and loose. A trig point stands at the top of Goat Fell, and the views are incredible on a clear day.

As with all walks, care must be taken in observing weather forecasts before setting off. Conditions can quickly and unexpectedly change, as Helen and I discovered on the second time we climbed Goat Fell. We got caught in an unexpected blizzard as we left the summit. Thankfully we were well equipped for such an event but the descent became rather trickier. We were glad to reach the Brewery, and even more so when we discovered it was still open - my personal preference is for an 'Isle of Arran Blonde'.

How to get there:

The start of the walk is a short distance north of Brodick, the island's capital.

51. Glenashdale

What you'll discover:

If ever there was a walk through history - from standing stones with burial cairns dating back millennia, to the site of a small Iron Age settlement - this is it. As well as the ancient history of the land, you also get stunning views and an amazing waterfall thrown in for good measure.

This circular walk starts in the village of Whiting Bay (originally Viking Bay), located in the southeast of the Isle of Arran. The route heads inland initially, and is signposted for Glenashdale Falls. Once in the woods there is an optional diversion to an Iron Age settlement, with an information board to tell you more.

Continuing on you will find Glenashdale Falls, easily the most impressive on the Isle of Arran. There are a couple of viewing platforms which give excellent photo opportunities. A short distance from the upper platform, you'll reach a forestry track that takes you to what are locally known as the 'Giant's Graves'. These clusters of large stones are not actually graves of giants, but are in fact ancient standing stones and burial cairns dating back to the third millennia BCE. When you are in this elevated position you get brilliant views across the Firth of Clyde, and over to Holy Island which is situated off the coast from Lamlash, the next village to the north of Whiting Bay. There is now a Buddhist Monastic settlement on Holy Island rather than a Christian one.

From the cairns the track heads downhill. Once at the bottom, follow the Glenashdale Burn back to Whiting Bay. You'll find some good options for sustenance in the village, and a nice art gallery.

The walk to Glenashdale Falls and back is a lovely route, and offers a great variety of scenery and history.

How to get there:

Whiting Bay sits on the main A841 road that goes all the way round the Isle of Arran. There is plenty of parking available in the village. The Coffee Pot cafe makes for a good starting point for this walk.

52. North Glen Sannox Pools and Falls

What you'll discover:

When you arrive at the car park of North Glen Sannox, the pools and falls are immediately obvious. There are literally dozens as you make your way along the path walking towards the plantation forest and beyond. As you walk up take the time to stop and enjoy the water pools and falls; as you wander further on they become more dramatic.

I was informed by a guide at the Isle of Arran distillery at Lochranza that the water on Arran is the purest in Scotland and therefore it makes the best whisky. Whether this was just a great sales pitch, or is actually true, the whisky produced is delicious and the water must play an important part.

Helen and I went gorge walking at North Glen Sannox in October 2016 as part of our honeymoon. We were the only ones brave (or daft) enough to book this adventure, perhaps not a surprise given the water temperature hit the heady heights of eight degrees Celsius (forty six Fahrenheit!). There were plenty of 'ice-cream headaches', cold toes, fingers and noses, but it was exhilarating and loads of fun. We felt a bit sorry for our water guide Kevin as he seemed to struggle a bit with the cold, but given that he was from much warmer climes in Australia we forgave him for his lack of hardiness - I'm sure he could handle heat far better than we could.

The walk simply continues as far as you wish, and follows the same path back to the car park. If you do decide to keep going you can incorporate some of Arran's more challenging mountain walks. Take a moment to sit next to one of the falls or pools - you may be tempted to jump in for a quick dook (swim), the water is very inviting whatever the weather.

How to get there:

There is a sizeable car park just off the main A841 road, approximately two miles north from the village of Sannox itself.

53. Elie Chain Walk

What you'll discover:

King James VI of Scots once described the Kingdom of Fife - which is a large peninsula of land located between the Firth of Forth to the north of Edinburgh and the Firth of Tay to the south of Dundee - as "a beggar's mantle fringed with gold". The fringe of gold refers to the beautiful coastline dotted with small scenic fishing villages. There is now a long distance walking trail in the form of the Fife Coastal Path which takes you from North Queensferry to Tayport, and encompasses many of these charming coastal settlements.

Interestingly it was from one of these fishing villages – Lower Largo – that a man by the name of Alexander Selkirk hailed from. Most people will never have heard of him by his real name but will certainly be more familiar with the name Robinson Crusoe, the character he inspired. In September 1704 Selkirk was marooned on the Isle of Juan Fernández, off the coast of Chile, for four years and four months before he was rescued. Once back in Britain, his story was discovered by the author Daniel Defoe and used as the inspiration for Defoe's famous character Crusoe. There is a statue in his home village of Lower Largo, just one example of the rich history and culture this area has to offer.

The Elie Chain Walk - an optional detour from the Fife Coastal Path - is a unique experience that I return to enjoy when I can. The object of this walk is to use a series of fixed chains over rocks, using them to follow the contours up, down, over and round various obstacles. The original chains were put in place by a local man in the 1920s, perhaps to aid local fishermen although the exact reason is not documented. They have subsequently been replaced by the council. The walk is an out and back - return via the chains if the tide allows or walk back over the cliffs.

Extreme caution should be taken when doing the walk, as its difficulty is governed by the tides. It is therefore essential that you check the tide times before you go. A level of physical fitness is required, as is a head for heights. The Elie Chain Walk gets your adrenaline pumping and proves that good outdoor exhilarating fun is better than any computer game.

How to get there:

The Elie Chain Walk is located on the section of the Fife Coastal Path between Lower Largo and Elie/Earlsferry. If travelling by car, there is on street parking near Earlsferry golf course. From there head down to the beach - the chain walk begins from the bottom of the cliffs just beyond the beach.

54. The Lomond Hills (Paps of Fife)

What you'll discover:

The word 'pap' meaning breast relates to the fact that the Lomond Hills - also known as the Paps of Fife - are two similarly sized rounded hills right next to each other. 'Lomond' comes from the Gaelic language, although some linguists would argue it is from the Brythonic/Pictish language. Regardless of the origin, it means 'beacon'.

Although the hills are not high they command incredible views over a huge area. On a clear day you can see right into the heart of the Cairngorm Mountains in the Highlands, Ben Lomond (another beacon hill) in the west, Soutra Hill in the Lammermuirs, plus much of the coastline stretching from the Bass Rock in East Lothian to Angus. The purpose of beacon hills was primarily for observation, and they also acted as an early warning system. If under attack or invasion from land or sea this is where you'd light your fires (or beacons) to warn the local population of approaching danger, whether it was from the Romans, Angles, Vikings or English.

The hills, East and West Lomond, can be climbed from the same car park, and it is worth exploring both for a greater sense of achievement and the fullest of views. The walks are on good paths and navigation is straightforward.

Once you've walked up the hills, head down to the pretty and historic nearby village of Falkland. There are a number of cafes available, and a couple of pubs should you wish for something stronger. You can also visit Falkland Palace and see one of the oldest surviving tennis courts in the world dating back nearly five hundred years. Here, the game of 'Real' (Royal) tennis was played, which resembled what is now squash. It was on the Falkland Palace tennis court where a bold Mary Queen of Scots turned up one day to play wearing 'trousers', apparently shocking the royal courtiers with her very unladylike behaviour and attire.

How to get there:

The start of the walk for both East and West Lomond is the Craigmeade car park, located a short distance south of Falkland.

55. Primrose Bay

What you'll discover:

Hopeman is a small former fishing village on the Moray (pronounced Murray) Coast. It sits on the Moray Coastal Trail, another walking route, and has a delightful setting. Hopeman is very close to Helen's heart as it was here that she and her family came for holidays. As children Helen and her brothers would spend endless summer days on the beach making sandcastles and swimming in the Moray Firth. Let's not forget that the Moray Firth is just another name for the North Sea which is not known for its subtropical temperatures - however on return from adventures in the surf the children would be rewarded for their bravery by what is referred to in Scotland as your 'chittery-bite'. As you eat your snack - usually something high in sugar - to help warm you up and replenish expended energy, your teeth chatter with the cold. Swimming in the Moray Firth could be viewed as a rather masochistic activity, but it was a good way of building character and gave Helen and her brothers a greater appreciation of the outdoors. To this day Helen prefers cooler temperatures and I put this down to her childhood holidays.

A mile or so along the Moray Coastal Trail to the east of Hopeman, there is a lovely spot called Cove Bay, or Clashach Bay, although it has always been referred to by Helen's family as Primrose Bay. There is a secluded beach with impressive rock formations all around. The local stone is prized for its colour and durability by sculptors all over the world. Whilst here, see if you can spot any dolphins cavorting out in the Moray Firth.

There is plenty to explore in this area of Scotland. Nearby you'll find historic Elgin Cathedral, Burghead Pictish site, and the interesting Findhorn community and eco-village. Let us not forget there's no lack of Scotland's national drink - whisky - in the nearby Speyside distilleries.

How to get there:

Hopeman is located not far from the A96 on the Moray Coast, six miles from Elgin.

56. Birks of Aberfeldy

What you'll discover:

The name 'birks' refers to the birch trees at Aberfeldy. The location was made famous by a poem of the same name written by Robert Burns (see treasure number 70). The wooded gorge gives you a sense of what much of the Highlands would have looked like before humans, sheep, and Norway spruce trees came along. There is a circular and very well waymarked walk that takes you into the fine gorge cut out by the River Moness, with lots of small scenic falls on the way, topped off with an impressive waterfall at the apex of the route. After the gorge ends, the River Moness runs down through the town of Aberfeldy into the River Tay, Scotland's longest river.

The name 'Aberfeldy' is interesting as it is Pictish in origin, with the 'aber' part meaning 'the confluence' or 'mouth of a river' (just like the word 'inver' in Gaelic), and the 'feldy' part most likely relating to a water sprite (faerie) that is supposed to have lived on or near the confluence of the Moness and the Tay. The faerie folk always chose well when it comes to places to stay.

Once you've had a good wander around the Birks, it's worth driving the short distance to the village of Kenmore on the banks of Loch Tay to visit the Scottish Crannog Centre. A crannog was an ancient circular dwelling built on a pontoon over water. You'll learn how ancient people lived in and around the numerous lochs and lochans of Scotland for thousands of years.

How to get there:

The car park for the Birks is located just to the south of Aberfeldy, on the A826 road for Crieff. If you decide to go to Kenmore follow the A827.

57. Birnam Oak and Birnam Hill

What you'll discover:

It's great to take the nice easy walk down to see the Birnam Oak on the banks of the River Tay. When people read or hear the word 'Birnam' they often think of Shakespeare's play 'Macbeth'. It is said that this oak tree has been here, quietly growing away, since Shakespeare's time. Experts think that the tree is over five hundred years old, which is old even for an oak. If you want to see the tree still standing I'd make haste to visit fairly soon because this old relic from the once great Birnam Wood (a non-fictional dense forest that was used against King Macbeth by the future Malcolm III) is seriously feeling the effects of its age.

If the walk to the Birnam Oak is too sedate, then get your boots on and take a walk up Birnam Hill. It is a short and sharp walk up but when you get to the top you get amazing views - to the north the Highlands and to the south the Central Lowlands. Birnam Hill sits right on the geographical Highland line that cuts across Scotland at a rough forty-five degree angle from Helensburgh in the west to Stonehaven in the east.

The walk is a loop and you can go either way, but be warned if you go up the north side first it is a steep pull and there is no time to let the legs warm up. Alternatively wander round to the south side, initially following the line of the railway, and take the steadier southern approach, although there are still some steep sections to negotiate. Thankfully there are steps, which is not the case on the north approach. Whichever way you decide, take your time; enjoy the woods, views, and the occasional natural spring en route. Once you're back in Birnam itself, grab a bite to eat in the Birnam Arts and

Conference Centre - the haggis filled baked potatoes come highly recommended.

Whilst in the area I'd recommend going to visit Dunkeld with its beautiful old Cathedral and grounds on the banks of the River Tay, which are worth the detour alone, but the actual village itself - technically city due to the presence of the Cathedral - is also lovely.

How to get there:

Birnam is located just off the A9 trunk road, around twelve miles north of Perth. The Birnam Oak is a short walk from the Oak Tree Inn towards the river. The Birnam Hill walk can be started from the Arts and Conference Centre, and there are information boards to assist with directions.

58. The Lost Valley

What you'll discover:

It is said by many that Glencoe is the epitome of the Western Highlands of Scotland. You are surrounded on all sides by dramatic and rugged mountainous scenery, which at one time - many millions of years ago - made up the outer edge of a giant super-volcano that lay to the south. Looking down the glen you can clearly make out the very distinctive 'U' shaped valley created by thousands of years of glacial movement.

Glencoe is arguably most famous for the 'Glencoe Massacre' - an awful event that occurred on Friday thirteenth of February 1692, when the MacDonalds of Glencoe were massacred in cold blood by a detachment of the Argyll Militia, the military arm of Clan Campbell, who had been staying with them.

There was an ancient Highland custom of hospitality that offered food and shelter in times of bad weather to anyone in need. This system of trust, which was understood and respected by everyone across the Highlands, was broken and abused by these militiamen, who had entered the glen eleven days earlier seeking protection from the weather. Little did the MacDonalds know that the soldiers had an ulterior motive. The massacre that occurred on the morning of the thirteenth was carried out to teach the MacDonalds a lesson for their chief being late in signing an oath of allegiance to King William of Orange. Thirty-eight people died that fateful morning, including women and children, and more perished due to the prevailing weather conditions as they ran for their lives.

Over the years the Campbell Clan were demonised for this brutal act against the MacDonalds but one must not forget who ordered the massacre, and who thought they would benefit the most from teaching the Highland Clans a lesson. In all likelihood the finger of blame can be directed at a man called John Dalrymple of Stair who was in effect King William of Orange's man in Scotland at the time. John was acting in a manner to try and curry favour with the new King. This is a complex moment in the history of Scotland, and it is certainly worth reading more about.

The massacre shocked the general public, particularly in the more genteel Lowlands but also across the Highlands. The abuse of the ancient custom of Highland hospitality was just as shocking as the lives lost. It is the escapees who fled into the snow on that tragic morning that we follow on this tricky but very rewarding walk.

The Lost Valley - known in Gaelic as 'Coire Gabhail' meaning 'the hollow of capture' - is a spectacular hidden gully where it is said the MacDonalds would hide their stolen cattle. It was here that they ran in the dark, mostly barefoot, when the sound of musket shots began to ring out around the glen on the morning of the massacre. Coire Gabhail has a very special feel about it - if rocks could speak you wonder what stories they would tell. The walk here is challenging but steeped in history.

How to get there:

Car parking is provided in the glen just off the A82. The Lost Valley sits between two of the Three Sisters of Glencoe. Once you have parked walk down into the glen, cross the small river and then veer off to the left. The path is easy to follow but can be rough and steep in places. Return is by the same path.

59. The Ringing Stone

What you'll discover:

The Isle of Tiree is well worth a visit because it is completely different from so much of the scenery that you find on the Western Isles of Scotland. It is a very flat island - there are next to no 'real' hills. For someone used to seeing obvious natural landmarks in the landscape, such as hills or mountains, and using them as a point of reference I found myself constantly getting disorientated.

Given Tiree's location and geography, there is no getting away from the fact that it is a windy place. No matter which direction the wind is coming from it's hard to avoid, but for many visitors it is this constant wind that they seek because Tiree is a surfer's paradise and is often described as 'the Hawaii of the north'. There are pristine beaches all around the island, and as well as being a great place to surf, it is also has lots of places to go snorkelling. The waters around the island are brilliantly clear and are warmed by the Gulf Stream. Although in no way as warm as the Caribbean where the Gulf Stream originates, Tiree is bathed in more hours of sunshine than much of the west coast and mainland of Scotland.

There is a lot to see and do on Tiree but a must is the walk to the intriguing Ringing Stone. It is a large boulder that doesn't belong as the rock type is not found on Tiree but originates on Mull. This stone was either pushed here by glaciers or - according to local folklore - a giant threw it. The walk begins from Vaul, and initially you pass by the ruins of Vaul Broch, which dates back to the first century AD. When you reach the Ringing Stone, on first impressions there is nothing particularly special, but pick up a stone, tap it on the boulder, and you will hear a metallic ringing sound.

When Helen and I went to the Ringing Stone we were initially underwhelmed. A kind lady who was doing some painting nearby told us what to do, and when we heard the chiming sound we were very impressed. To the ancient people of Tiree, the Ringing Stone would have been something special, perhaps something ceremonial, and even today it has a certain feel about it that is hard to describe. Tap the stone and see how it makes you feel.

How to get there:

There is one main road of sorts that takes you around Tiree and from that main road all others branch off. Vaul is located on the north easterly side and is easily found on a map of the island.

60. The Table, Quiraing

What you'll discover:

The Trotternish peninsula on the north east of the Isle of Skye is unique for one main reason - its ridge. The ridge is an enormous landslip that has been created over thousands of years. It is the longest and largest of its kind to be found in the British Isles, and features amazing and unique landscapes.

The two most famous features on the ridge are the Old Man of Storr, which is a very impressive pinnacle of rock, and the Quiraing. Many would say that the Quiraing - 'the round folded rock' in Old Norse - is hardly a hidden treasure given its location, size and popularity. However, many visitors only travel as far as the car park and enjoy what is, it has to be said, a spectacular and iconic view. This treasure goes a bit further - it is the view from *within* the Quiraing that is so special.

The Table, as the name suggests, is a flat piece of ground that cannot be seen from the path below or from a distance - the only way to get to this amazing place is to walk there. The walk is pretty straightforward, heading left from the car park as you look back down the road to Staffin. There are some slightly tricky bits to negotiate but nothing too difficult. As you walk along you can see some impressive remnants of the landslip, including features such as 'the Needle' and 'the Prison'. As you pick your way up you'll have to negotiate through rugged crevasses - at times it feels like you are entering another world. Keep following the path and soon you'll find the Table - it is the only flat bit of land.

All around you like an amphitheatre the volcanic rock juts up in menacing dark grey outcrops giving a real sense of being enclosed in this otherworldly place. Occasionally a raven gives out a guttural croak which just helps add extra effect to your experience. Stay a while to explore and then return the way you came.

How to get there:

The Quiraing is located near the village of Staffin on the east of the Trotternish peninsula, a short distance from the A855 road. Parking is found at the main viewpoint.

61. Rubha Hunish

What you'll discover:

Rubha Hunish, 'the headland of the bear cub', is a spectacular walk at the very top of the Trotternish peninsula in the north of the Isle of Skye. The origin of the name is interesting as it combines Gaelic - 'Rubha' means headland - and Old Norse - 'Huna' means bear cub. It may relate to the existence of bears here - at one time there were many in Scotland - or it may have been a nickname given to a Viking settler.

Thankfully there are no bears here now to worry about, although at certain times of year it is a favoured spot for whale watching. If you ever want to get that feeling of getting away from it all without having to go very far then this is the walk for you. As you drive up the Trotternish peninsula, the scenery is like a film set, and in fact it has been used in popular films like 'Highlander' from the 1980s and 'Prometheus' in 2012.

The walk to Rubha Hunish is straightforward although some parts of the track can be boggy. On the way you'll see the remnants of a settlement of blackhouses called Erisco. As you look across Tulm Bay you can see the ruins of Duntulm Castle, the former seat of the MacDonalds of Skye. Make sure you don't miss the old coastguard lookout which is now cared for by the Mountain Bothies Association - it is possible to bunk down for a night and donations are always welcome for the upkeep. It is also nice to stop in for a quick break if the need arises to get out of the weather. There are amazing three hundred and sixty degree views all around and you'll understand why this is a favoured place for wildlife spotting.

Below the lookout the headland of Rubha Hunish is visible. To explore this stretch of land, a tricky path takes you down. It is quite steep to begin with but does improve as you venture on. As you walk around the headland there are small inlets where the sea atmospherically crashes in, sea stacks, and an arch to admire. The most northerly point on the Isle of Skye is a truly spectacular place, and if you are visiting on a nice day you can spend hours exploring.

How to get there:

Near the Duntulm Hotel and castle ruins, there is a small signpost pointing for Shulista. A short distance from the road there is a small car park with an information board, and it is from here that you start the walk.

62. Stac Pollaidh

What you'll discover:

In older reference maps, this mountain is referred to as 'An Stac' which means 'the pinnacle'. More recently, it has come to be known as Stac Pollaidh (pronounced polly) meaning 'the pinnacle of the pool river', or 'peak of the peat moss'. It is located in the North West Highlands in an area called Assynt, easily one of the most spectacular and dramatic parts of Scotland. It is because of the unique landscapes found in and around Assynt that this area became part of the network of UNESCO Global Geoparks, which are locally run projects designed to promote sustainable development of a sensitive area through geotourism.

Stac Pollaidh is classified as a Graham, a mountain between two and two and a half thousand feet high, with at least four hundred and ninety feet of descent on all sides. Although it is not the highest mountain in the area, it is certainly one of the more accessible. The circular path is in good condition. Helen and I went up around the eastern shoulder, with a push up to the top from the rear northern side. On arrival on the ridge you are met with jaw-dropping views of the surrounding mountains and landscape, with the Atlantic Ocean to the west.

When standing admiring the view, imagine for a moment the same place over ten thousand years ago. You would have found yourself on a glacial island - referred to as a 'Nunatak' - completely surrounded by ice with only a few of the other high peaks in the area visible.

The pinnacles along the ridge are similar to those found at the Table on the Quiraing (treasure number 60) and the Old Man of Storr on the Isle of Skye.

There are two summit points; the one on the eastern side is lower and less tricky to get up to, whereas the one on the western side is much more demanding, and scrambling skills and a good head for heights are required. When you descend, continue with the circuit and follow the track back down. Due to Helen and I's over-purchasing of pies at Lochinver Larder (treasure number 42), we had a great feast on our return to the car park, a fitting way to end an amazing walk in an impressive landscape.

How to get there:

From the A835 road between Ullapool and Ledmore, turn off at Drumrunie following signs for Achnahaird. The walk starts and finishes from a car park on the shores of Loch Lurgainn.

63. Steall Falls and the Nevis Gorge

What you'll discover:

This is a relatively short yet dramatic walk up and along the Nevis Gorge, located in the shadow of Scotland's highest mountain Ben Nevis, which is one thousand three hundred and forty-five metres in height. The word 'steall' is Gaelic for waterfall, and 'nevis' has a couple of possible meanings; either 'venomous' or 'being in the clouds/heavens'. Both are plausible given that the top of Ben Nevis is often shrouded in cloud and can be a dangerous mountain to climb.

As you follow the path up the gorge you get the feeling of walking through an ancient landscape with old twisted, gnarly Scots Pines looming over you. Parts of the gorge walk are not for those who suffer from vertigo as there are steep drops down to the River Nevis below. However one of the benefits of your elevated position is that there are great views looking towards Glen Nevis.

Once you are beyond the gorge, the land opens out into what is called the Steall plain - you are surrounded by awesome mountain scenery on all sides and in the distance you can see the Steall Falls. If you wish to get right up close and personal with the falls then you are required to cross the Nevis River by means of a wire rope bridge, involving a balanced shimmy across the water. This adds to the adventure and fun of being out in such an amazing place. Simply head back the same way you came.

How to get there:

To the north of Fort William town centre, turn off the main A82 onto a smaller road signposted for Glen Nevis. Continue along this road as far as it will go. When you get to the end there is a car park, where the walk begins.

Sites of Historic Interest and Intrigue

Scotland has such a wide variety of historic sites. In this final section I take you on a journey to discover some very unique and special places that reflect this variety. From larger-than-life maps and horse heads, emotive battlefields, mysterious man-made caves, ancient megaliths, and cutting edge design, these treasures are truly intriguing and thought-provoking.

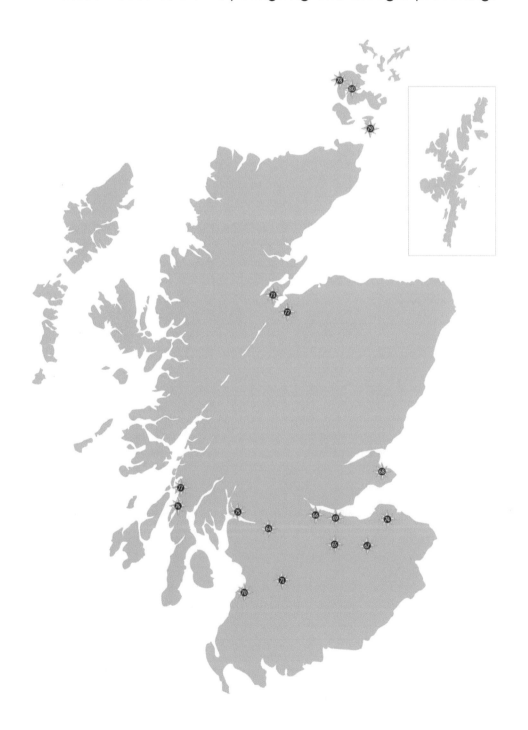

64. The Govan Stones

What you'll discover:

Mention Govan to most Scots and they will either think of the once industrious shipbuilding yards on the banks of the River Clyde, or the home of Glasgow Rangers Football Club. Govan is also one of the many post-industrial areas of Scotland that is currently undergoing massive regeneration. What doesn't jump into people's minds is what is found inside Govan Old Parish Church. Here, one of the finest collections of ninth to eleventh century early medieval carved stones, which are totally unique from a Scottish perspective, are on display. At Govan, the current church is the last in a long line of Christian buildings to have been built on the same site going back over one and half millennia.

On display there are interesting shafts of what would have been Celtic crosses with fine intricate knotwork on them, and ornately carved stone slabs. However, the stand out artifacts are the Viking hogbacks stones, and an ancient stone sarcophagus of St Constantine. The hogbacks are very rare, and what is fascinating is that although they are viewed as being Viking in origin, hogback stones are not found anywhere in Scandinavia. It seems that this particular stone craftsmanship was unique to the Vikings that conquered and settled in Britain. Some resemble the longhouses of Danish chiefs from the tenth century, whereas others are more serpent-like in appearance. There are also hogbacks that are viewed as hybrids between Christian and Pagan (a term I don't like using because it has belittling undertones) beliefs, showing that the Vikings were beginning to adopt Christianity. It is commonly agreed amongst historians that hogback stones were grave markers/covers made for important warriors or chiefs. According to some historic sources, they were of a style that only lasted for around fifty years which adds to their rareness. The only other place where hogbacks have been found in such concentration is Yorkshire in England, and although very similar in design they are smaller in size.

The sarcophagus of St Constantine dates from an earlier time than the hogback stones, and is even rarer. There has been some disagreement as to which Constantine the sarcophagus is dedicated to, but scholars seem fairly sure it is King Constantine I of Alba, who ruled from the mid to late ninth century. Although the sarcophagus was located in the ancient kingdom of Strathclyde in the heartlands of the Britons, the designs are distinctly Pictish with possibly some Norse influences. What the sarcophagus demonstrates is that although the Picts and the Britons were often adversaries, the symbology of power was the same - shown through the hunting scenes carved on the sides. Another unique element of the sarcophagus is that it was carved from one piece of stone and this is seen nowhere else in Scotland.

The stones and the church are very interesting - when I visited a volunteer took me on an informal guided tour of the exhibition.

How to get there:

Govan Old Parish Church is located at 866 Govan Road, Glasgow, and is open from 1pm-4pm every day between the first of April and the thirty-first of October. The exhibition is free to visit although donations are welcome. Visit www.thegovanstones.org.uk for more information.

65. The Great Polish Map of Scotland

What you'll discover:

The Barony Map, as it is sometimes called, is one of the 80 treasures in this book that actually is a 'world's largest'! Yes that's right, the Great Polish Map of Scotland (as it is more commonly known now) is the largest terrain relief model in the world, and was the creation of Jan Tomasik. The map is a three dimensional model of mainland Scotland and the Western Isles, and measures fifty metres long and forty metres wide. Unfortunately it doesn't include the northern Isles of Orkney and Shetland.

Jan came to Scotland from Poland during the Second World War. When the war was over he decided to stay in his newly adopted country, and he entered into the hospitality industry. He bought the Barony Castle Hotel (or Black Barony as it was at the time) in 1968. The map is said to have been inspired by a visit he made to Brussels in 1958 where he saw a similar map of Belgium at the Brussels World's Fair. The building of the map fell to his Polish wartime friends, one of whom - Maczek - had been his Army General. They made the 1:10,000 model using bricks and concrete over six summers between 1974 and 1979. The hotel changed hands in the mid 1980s, and the map was sadly allowed to deteriorate to the point where it was no longer visible due to vegetation.

©Craig Allardyce
@csa_adventure

Thankfully money secured from various charitable sources between 2010 and 2013 has ensured the map's future. It has now been fully restored, including having water in some of the lochs and surrounding coastline, and a viewing platform has been erected to give a good overall perspective from what would be Cumbria in the north of England. It really is a splendid creation, and according to Tomasik it was his gift to the Scottish people for their hospitality during the war years. We can all raise a glass to that sentiment.

How to get there:

Located near the main A703 road between Peebles and Edinburgh is the village of Eddleston. From the road, follow the signs for the Barony Castle Hotel and the Great Polish Map. Park in the hotel car park, walk to the left hand side of the hotel, and follow the signs for 'Maczek's map'.

66. The Kelpies

What you'll discover:

What is a Kelpie? This treasure relates to two equine structures, however to understand the name 'the Kelpies' we must firstly examine the legend of the water horse.

Scotland can be (at times) a very wet country. Let us go back to a time when people were incredibly superstitious, and were rarely taught how to swim. As beautiful and life-giving as water is, it is also very dangerous in equal measure. It is with this danger in mind that we find the origins of the numerous Kelpie legends found across Scotland.

Legend has it that Kelpies were dangerous creatures that inhabited dark waters - be that a river pool, a loch, or even the open sea. The Kelpie would appear from its watery home and stand near the water's edge taking the form of a stunning glistening horse. The idea was to lure children (or possibly young ill-informed adults) into the water, where before they knew it, they would be carried out to be consumed by the Kelpie. However, there were certain organs the Kelpie didn't like to eat apparently, the most disagreeable parts being the lungs and - depending on the legend - the heart.

Some historians say that the origins of the Loch Ness monster legend began with St Columba using his cross of Christ and some harsh words to banish a Kelpie back into the dark depths of the loch after it tried to take one of his Christian followers. A story such as this demonstrated the power of Christianity over long held superstitions and thus aided the expansion of this new religion across Scotland. Odd as this story may sound, near the village of Achnasheen in the Highlands there is a 'Loch Sgamhain' which means 'Loch of the Lungs', relating to a gruesome local legend of a man being lured and eaten by a resident Kelpie. A few days later the victim's lungs were found at the loch's edge. Scary stuff!

Thankfully today the Kelpies that you can visit aren't going to lure you into the water, and one can admire the largest equine structures in the world, each standing at thirty metres in height. Each individual component part that makes up the skin of the Kelpies is unique, adding to the engineering brilliance that has gone into their creation. Completed in October 2013, they are the main part of a regeneration project called the Helix and were the brainchild of a Scottish sculptural artist called Andy Scott. They are based on two real life Clydesdale horses (Scottish working horses) called Baron and Duke, although sadly Baron died in January 2017 from colic.

It was from this type of working horse and their strength that we have the unit of power we call horsepower today. The term was first coined by James Watt (inventor of the separate condenser that made steam engines work more efficiently) when he was trying to convey the power of his new, more efficient, steam-powered pump engine to mine owners who didn't understand the technical data he was presenting to them. But they did understand saving money and what a horse could pull, hence the use of the term 'horsepower'.

When visiting the Kelpies, you can take a tour to see the inside of these amazing structures and learn more about them.

How to get there:

The Kelpies and Helix project are easily found just off the M9 motorway between Edinburgh and Stirling at Falkirk. There is ample parking available.

67. Soutra Aisle

What you'll discover:

It is hard to believe that on a windswept and slightly bleak hillside set in the Lammermuir Hills there was at one time a hospital of great renown. Not a modern hospital all white, clinical and shiny of course, but the largest medieval hospital in Scotland. The House of the Holy Trinity, as it was called then, was founded in 1164 by Malcolm IV, and run by monks from the Augustinian order. Due to the monk's religious connections throughout Britain and beyond onto the continent, the hospital had an impressive reputation as a great place of healing. During excavations, over two hundred different types of medicinal herbs and seeds were found including the opium poppy.

The hospital was located on the main trunk road heading north and south referred to as the Via Regia, or 'King's Road', which in turn followed the line of the much more ancient Roman Road called Dere Street. Being located on a main travel route would have also helped spread its reputation. With the name 'King's Road' you can see where George R.R. Martin got some of his inspiration for his massively popular books and subsequent television series 'Game of Thrones'.

It is amazing to think that virtually nothing remains of what must have been quite a complex series of buildings, but there are some very good information panels to help with interpretation. Today all that can be seen is a small family burial aisle that was used by the Pringle family. Although the history of this place is fascinating, another reason for stopping is to admire the view looking north. As you scan around it is easy to pick out natural features such as North Berwick Law, the Firth of Forth, the Paps of Fife, the Ochil Hills, and the Highland line with its mountainous terrain lying beyond. On a clear day it is remarkable how far the eye can see.

How to get there:

Whether you are travelling on the A68 or the A7, Soutra Aisle is easy to find. From the A68 it is around half a mile from the turnoff onto the B6368, and from the A7 it is around four miles from the turnoff signposted for Gilston.

68. Dunino Den

What you'll discover:

On my first visit to Dunino Den I thought I'd walked onto the film set of the Blair Witch Project. It was a cold damp day in early November 2002 not long after the Samhain (also known as the Celtic New Year and nowadays as Halloween), and I didn't really know what I was looking for. As I initially entered the wide and well forested gully, still unsure of what it was I was supposed to find, all of a sudden a murder of crows went crazy in the trees above me, only to then a moment later fall deathly silent. The sudden silence added to my sense of unease. It was then that I noticed many trinkets and small personal offerings tied into the trees; my imagination began to run wild with images of sinister Pagan rituals and I had a very real sense that I was being watched. After my initial over-reaction had subsided, and I had visited on numerous other occasions as well as reading more about it, I discovered that there is a lot more to Dunino Den than meets the eye.

There is nothing sinister about the place at all, although there is a sense of something 'otherworldly', and definitely an energy that is hard to describe. It is likely that Dunino Den has been used for millennia as a site of spiritual significance and worship long before there was any form of Christianity in the area. It is often referred to as being a Pictish site (the Picts are talked about in more detail in treasure number 6) and indeed there were some Pictish carved stones found in the nearby churchyard, but it is likely the site pre-dates the Picts as well.

When you walk in from the direction of the church through the trees, you find a raised outcrop of rock which is almost altar-like in its appearance with a footprint carved into it (the significance of the footprint is discussed at treasure number 16), next to a circular pool/well. There is a sense that a priest or druid could easily have stood here and been observed from all around with reverence. Although there are some similarities between the two ceremonial sites of Dunino Den and Dunadd Hill Fort, there is one key difference in that Dunadd was a heavily fortified site with rings of defensive ramparts - Dunino Den has no signs of being extensively defended.

From 'the altar', for want of a better description, descend down the narrow, roughly cut steps to the flat area next to the Dunino Burn. This is where you tend to find the majority of offerings that people have left. There are some carvings found on the exposed stone surfaces, one of which appears to be the remnants of a Celtic cross and another is a Celtic knot. The knot looks like it has been carved a lot more recently than the cross. The cross appears to be much more ancient in origin judging by the weathering it has suffered.

Dunino Den brims with atmosphere so stay awhile and enjoy it.

How to get there:

Dunino is a tiny hamlet located between St Andrews and Anstruther on the B9131. There is no sign to direct you to Dunino Den but there is a small sign to Dunino Church. Park on the gravel next to the church and walk down the grassy path in-between the old and new cemeteries. Once you pass through two gates you will notice a gap in the stone wall ahead. Walk through the gap and follow the rough path for around twenty metres.

69. Gilmerton Cove

What you'll discover:

Located on the southern edge of Scotland's capital city of Edinburgh - with all its splendid Georgian architecture, fascinating museums and galleries, Castle, Palace of Holyroodhouse and many more attractions for visitors to enjoy - is the suburb of Gilmerton. In amongst old miners' cottages, modern housing developments and food takeaways, we find our next treasure - although you'd be forgiven for thinking why on earth am I here...

It is below the cottages, and indeed the main road, that we need to go. The entrance into Gilmerton Cove is via one of the cottages at street level, and a bit of forward planning is required as you need to make an appointment to visit. However, it is certainly worth the effort.

The cove is a series of man-made underground chambers and tunnels. The purpose of these remains a mystery. That is where the cove guides help to stimulate your thoughts and imagination, although the eerie nature of the place does its own inspiring. Some say it was an illicit drinking den used by the gentry; perhaps it was a smugglers store; others say a refuge for people to avoid religious persecution; or was it possibly used for something much more sinister and occult? Maybe all of the above...

The mystery and intrigue that surrounds the cove is what first caught my attention, and the uniqueness of the experience means it stands out as a visitor attraction. There's certainly something that draws people in - in 2012 it outranked all other attractions across Edinburgh and reached the top spot on Tripadvisor. You'd think with all this kudos and gravitas that it would be swamped by people but thankfully this is not the case, and a visit to the cove is highly rewarding.

How to get there:

Gilmerton Cove is located at 16 Drum Street, a continuation of Gilmerton Road which heads south from Edinburgh on the A772. Parking can be a bit tricky but there is some to be found nearby on Ravenscroft Street. Alternatively use the local public buses and jump on either the number 3 or 29, both of which stop nearby. To visit is by appointment only, and details can be found on the website.

70. The Robert Burns Birthplace Museum

What you'll discover:

Robert Burns is arguably one of the best known Scots of all time. His birth and works are celebrated the world over every year on Burns Night, the twenty-fifth of January, and also on Hogmanay (New Year) when people from across the globe sing 'Auld Lang Syne'.

'Rabbie' was a man of great depth, perception, and feeling towards his fellow humans and his nation, but like us all he wasn't perfect and on occasion his appreciation of the fairer sex got him into a bit of trouble. His clever use of hidden - or not so hidden - double entendres was brilliant. For example, in his poem 'Address to a Haggis', he is not only installing the virtues of the humble offal-filled savoury pudding, but also reminding his fellow Scots not to disregard what they have and see it as inferior, but to celebrate it. In 'To a Mouse' he talks of a small field mouse being cast from its simple dwelling and having to flee in fear of the beating paddle of the farmer. This act of being brutally thrown out and cast asunder is a reflection of the lack of security that many rural people suffered, and the fear that they too could be thrown from their land and homes at the whim of a landowner, feelings that Burns himself could relate to.

Burns was also a much more complicated man than many would have him be recognised for. In one of his most famous poems, 'A Man's A Man For A' That', he rails against privilege, and describes how a man's worth is not found in his clothes, belongings and titles, but in the strength of his character, and that all mankind are equal the world over. These thoughts and ideals still hold true to this day, but ironically it was through people of privilege that Burns became known and popular, as they helped to promote him as a recognised poet of worth and reputation. Let us also not forget that before he became famous he had seriously considered going to the colonies of the Caribbean to become a bookkeeper on a slave plantation, which completely contradicts the ideals of equality he promoted, however a person is allowed to change their opinion. Above all, Burns was a human being and he, like all of us, had his greatness and his flaws. However his ability to find popularity across society from the duke's son to the cook's son was no mean feat for his day.

The best way to learn about this amazingly talented human is to go to where it all started for him in his home village of Alloway. The Robert Burns Birthplace Museum is full of information on the life and works of Burns, and really brings to life this great man and his literary achievements. Whilst visiting take the short walk from the Alloway Auld Kirk (just down the road from Burn's Cottage) and follow the road down to the Brig o' Doon - this is the same path that Rabbie's ill-fated character Tam O'Shanter rode for his life to escape pursuing witches.

Burns took inspiration and delight from simple everyday things and people, and in that there is a lesson to us all.

How to get there:

Alloway was a village up until 1935 but is now a suburb of Ayr. The A77 runs right past the town but you need turn off onto Doonholm Road - the Museum and Cottage are located on Murdoch's Loan, and are well signposted from the A77. Both are in the care of the National Trust for Scotland, and there is an admission charge.

71. St Bride's Kirk

What you'll discover:

Many people around the world are familiar with the popular 1995 film Braveheart. It was an entertaining Hollywood interpretation of an epic poem called 'The Wallace', written by a Scots makar (poet/bard) referred to as 'Blind Harry' (who wasn't actually blind but was called Harry). Harry is said to have written or developed this poem in the late fifteenth century (most likely around 1480, more than one hundred and seventy-five years after William Wallace's time), and it is recognised by many Scottish historians as having a fair bit of poetic licence interwoven with some historical fact. Braveheart was based on Harry's version of events, thus it was also not entirely historically accurate, but let's be honest, we don't go to the cinema to be educated, and by adding the heroic title its audience appeal was sealed.

However the real story of 'Braveheart' relates to St Bride's Kirk and the loyal right hand man of King Robert the Bruce, the Good Sir James Douglas. James allied himself with Robert early in his campaign to become King of Scots, and stuck by him through all the highs and lows that were to come during the Scottish Wars of Independence, remaining his loyal friend right to the end of Robert's life. Previous to meeting and joining Bruce, James had lost all his land entitlement due to his father's support for William Wallace, and bore a great grudge against Edward I of England, and the English in general, for his unsatisfactory situation. By throwing his lot in with Bruce he had nothing to lose and everything to gain. James proved to be a fearless, brutal and incredibly ruthless warrior. The mere mention of his name would strike fear into his enemy's hearts, earning him the nickname 'The Black Douglas'.

It was in Sir James's final act that we find the true origin of the legend of Braveheart. One of Robert the Bruce's last verbal requests was that his heart be taken on a crusade against the enemies of Christianity (i.e. the Moors in Spain), although some say he requested that his heart be presented at the Holy Sepulchre in Jerusalem to atone for his sins (this is less likely as Islamic rulers had held Jerusalem since 1187). During the Battle of Teba (in what is nowadays Andalucia in the south of Spain) on the twenty-fifth of August 1330, James was facing a moment of certain death. It is said that in that moment he removed the casket containing Bruce's heart, which he'd been carrying around his neck, and threw it into the fray, shouting the words "Lead on my braveheart; I followed you in life and shall now follow you in death!" - or words to that effect because there are differing accounts of events and nobody is totally sure what he shouted - if anything at all! Ultimately in this final heroic act, the legend of the Good Sir James Douglas was cemented.

James's heart and bones were brought back to Scotland by Sir William Keith and Sir Simon Lockhart, and entombed at the family church of St Bride's in Douglas, which now contains the mausoleum to the Black Douglases (as the descendants of Sir James became known after his death).

The oldest part of the church dates back to the 1100s, although much of what you can see today dates from the late 1300s. On entering there is a real sense of awe - James's heart is now sealed in a lead heart-shaped casket which is set into the floor beneath a glass panel. There is also an effigy to the Good Sir James along with others from the Black Douglas family. It is quite a remarkable place, and the canopied tombs are amongst the most important of their kind in Scotland. During a visit you'll also be able to see Scotland's oldest working clock dating from 1565, and there is a pleasant walk to 'Castle Dangerous', a local folly which was part of Douglas Castle at one time, a short distance from the Kirk.

How to get there:

The village of Douglas is located on the A70, a short distance from the M74 motorway. On entering the village, turn right at the first mini-roundabout and park on the street outside St Bride's Kirk. The Kirk is in the care of Historic Environment Scotland, via a local custodian, and although open all year round opening times do vary depending on the availability of the key-keeper, so it is essential to call ahead in advance of visiting on 01555 851657.

72. Culloden Battlefield

What you'll discover:

Culloden - or Drummossie Muir as it was originally known - is a battle that has often been misrepresented and misunderstood by many over the years. Thankfully today there is a very comprehensive visitor centre at the battlefield site which explains the complicated and intricate history from all the various points of view held at the time. The men fighting on both sides were there for many different reasons including - religious belief; seeking revenge for previous battlefield humiliation; looking to dissolve the Treaty of Union between the Scottish and English parliaments; loyalty to a particular line of monarchy; the preservation of the clan system that was under threat - the centre does well to explain these varied standpoints.

The Battle of Culloden, which took place on the sixteenth of April 1746, lasted under an hour but its consequences were far reaching and are still felt to this day throughout the Highlands, and beyond Scotland's shores. The battle was a culmination of a series of five uprisings and rebellions, referred to as 'the Jacobite Rebellions', in the attempt to put the deposed House of Stuart (originally Stewart) back on the throne of Britain and Ireland. On one side you had Charles Edward Stuart - also referred to as the 'Young Pretender' (pretender deriving from 'pretandre' in French, meaning claimant) - and on the opposing side his cousin Prince William, Duke of Cumberland, leading the Government forces on behalf of the House of Hanover. The Jacobites (meaning supporters of James, Charles's grandfather, whose removal from the throne in 1688 triggered the rebellions) were outnumbered and outgunned. They fought heroically in tough weather and ground conditions, adopting the infamous 'Highland Charge'; however their weapons - more suited for hand to hand combat - were no match for the horrendous grapeshot and cannon fire from the Hanoverian forces.

The aftermath of Culloden had a brutal effect upon the Highlands - the subsequent Act of Proscription made it illegal to wear tartan and Highland dress, the distilling of whisky was banned, the Gaelic language was outlawed, and clan chiefs no longer held any power. The ancient clan system was no more. The Highland Clearances that followed later in the century and into the nineteenth century occurred as a direct consequence of the battle (discussed more in treasure number 76).

It is essential to go through the visitor centre before going onto the battlefield in order to get a much better understanding of a complicated period of history.

On one occasion I met an Australian couple in Inverness who had visited Culloden that day with their three year old daughter. Once they had gone through the visitor centre and were out exploring the battlefield, the little girl turned to her mother and said "Mummy, why are all the men lying on the ground?"

I still get shivers when I remember hearing the couple recount what their daughter said.

How to get there:

Culloden Battlefield is located on the B9006, around ten minutes drive from the A9. The visitor centre is operated by the National Trust for Scotland and there is an admission charge.

73. The Clootie Well

What you'll discover:

When I first visited the Clootie Well, my reaction was "what on earth is this place...it's pretty cool though."

The Clootie Well (originally called St Curetán's Well, then St Boniface's Well) is a sacred well which is said to have magical healing properties. A piece of cloth ('cloot' in the Scots tongue), or garment (if you have an ailment that is covered by that particular garment, such as a sock in the case of a sore foot), is soaked in the water of the well, whilst making a wish or prayer, then the material is tied to the branches of a tree. The belief is that the wind dries the cloth and takes your prayer, or request for a cure, to Mother Earth in the hope that your wish is answered positively, or that a cure is forthcoming for your ailment. This simple and symbolic ritual dates back millennia, and is still undertaken today.

Similar to my experience at Dunino Den I was completely unaware of what the well represented when I first visited. It gives us a glimpse back into an ancient belief system. Long before we had access to modern sanitation, having a clean reliable source of water available wasn't easy - when you had one you cherished it. Today for many of us living in the western - and arguably overly-sanitised world - we take clean water running from our taps for granted. Clean water is crucial to life, but it also has a power to help us heal and rejuvenate both bodily and spiritually. Given that most of the human body is made up of water it seems only natural and sensible that we enjoy this spiritual connection. Thus water sources such as the Clootie Well became places of great importance for both practical and spiritual reasons.

Although some may be sceptical, the Clootie Well still resonates as a special place and is worthy of being a treasure because it demonstrates a belief system that goes back thousands of years.

On arrival at the well, dip a cloot (or spill three drops on the ground), make a wish and see how Mother Nature responds...

How to get there:

The Clootie Well is situated on the B9161 near Munlochy, in the area known as the Black Isle (although it is not an island!), north of Inverness. There is a car park provided for safe access.

74. Traprain Law

What you'll discover:

As mentioned in the introduction, this book is not about finding hidden treasure in the dictionary definition of the word, however for those lucky enough actual treasure has been found in some of these locations. At the top of Traprain Law, the site of a hill fort in East Lothian, a hoard of ancient Roman silver was unearthed in 1919 during an archaeological dig. It consisted of around twenty-six kilograms of silver trinkets, plates, bowls and coins. Some artifacts had been hacked into smaller pieces, possibly into weights of silver recognised in the Roman world for trading with at a time when there was a shortage of coins (due to the Roman withdrawal from Brittania in the early fifth century). Other artifacts remained intact.

Exactly why this hoard was here is still open to debate, and is a bit of a mystery. Some say it was payment for mercenary services rendered, or maybe it was some form of blackmail payment to the chief of the Gododdin, the incumbent tribe (although the Romans referred to them as the Votadini), to prevent them raiding south of Hadrian's Wall. One thing is for sure, whoever buried it for safekeeping didn't live to retrieve it or tell anybody else about it. The artifacts are now on display at the National Museum of Scotland.

Silver treasure aside, Traprain Law is an ancient site. Archaeologists say that it was originally used for ceremonial burials from at least 1500 BCE, and became a fortified site around 1000 BCE, with the ramparts of the hill fort built and rebuilt many times over in the years during the Bronze Age into the Iron Age. It was at one time the capital of the Gododdin tribe who inhabited what is today the south east of Scotland and north east of England. The Gododdin had other fort sites including what is today Edinburgh Castle, and the site of Old Roxburgh Castle (treasure number 10), but the discovery of the silver proves the significance of Traprain.

It was in the skies above Traprain Law and East Lothian that the Scottish Flag, the Saltire, has its origin. During the Battle of Athelstaneford, not far from Traprain, in 832 CE, the King of the Picts Angus MacFergus (who had been doing a bit of summer raiding in the area to the south of Traprain, which by this time was part of the Kingdom of Northumbria), was losing the battle against Eanred of Northumbria. Things were getting desperate for Angus, and it is said that he looked into the sky for some sort of divine intervention (which he had been told he would receive in a dream the previous night) and lo and behold, he got it. Above him was blue sky and a cloud in the X-shape of the cross of St Andrew - a saint the Picts were very familiar with. In that moment he and all his men were inspired, and with this inspiration they killed all the Angles and King Eanred. In time St Andrew became Scotland's patron saint, and Scotland's national flag - with a white cross against a blue background - was born. This flag of Scotland is arguably the oldest, or at least one of the oldest, flags in the world.

Traprain Law ('law' meaning a rounded hill, or burial mound) involves a relatively easy climb up - once at the top you get fantastic views across the area of East Lothian and the Firth of Forth. There is normally a small herd of friendly (some may say over friendly) fell ponies found grazing.

How to get there:

Traprain Law is located between Haddington and East Linton. Park in the small lay-by provided and start your walk up from there.

75. Hill House

What you'll discover:

If you like modern art, a visit to Hill House - designed by Charles Rennie MacKintosh - is a must. Charles was born and brought up in Glasgow at a time of massive change to the city. It had become the centre of an innovative heavy engineering and shipbuilding industry, and Charles would have witnessed the growth of the city and its prosperity from this sector. The style of art that he created was a fusion of various influences - from his Scottish upbringing, he blended the practical thinking of the Scots with the flourish of the Art Nouveau movement, and coupled these ideas with the simplicity and elegance of Japanese forms.

Although it is the name Charles Rennie MacKintosh that we are most familiar with today, it should always be remembered that behind every great man there is an even greater woman. For Charles, that was his wife Margaret MacDonald. Each design Charles created came with extensive specifications for the finishing details, decoration, and furnishing of his buildings - these were almost entirely done by Margaret. Good design is one thing, but finishing it is another, and Charles and Margaret combined their talents to create something very special.

Hill House took all of MacKintosh's skill, clever design, and application of his ideas and principles to create a practical yet elegant home. He designed the house and nearly everything inside, from the decorative schemes and the furniture to the fittings and contents - with Margaret's help of course. Much of the house has been restored so it looks almost exactly as it did in 1904 when its first residents, the Glasgow publisher Walter Blackie and his family, moved in. Today it is looked after and maintained by the National Trust for Scotland.

Mackintosh's distinctive style is instantly recognisable and once seen it is never forgotten - many would say his style was ahead of its time and not fully appreciated whilst he was alive.

How to get there:

Hill House is located on Upper Colquhoun Street, Helensburgh. It is open in the summer season from 11.30am until 5.00pm, although it is a good idea to call in advance of your visit. There is an admission fee.

76. Arichonan Township

What you'll discover:

Following the Battle of Culloden (treasure number 72), there were massive repercussions that resonated throughout Scotland and beyond. What you see today at the clearance village of Arichonan Township is a direct result of that ripple effect.

The Clan system of the Highlands was an ancient tribal way of life; one in which family ties and bonds were sacred. Most people lived in relatively small communities and groupings called clachans (hamlets in English), working and living off the land, and raising their families. It was low-intensity pastoral farming, and anything produced over and above what was needed could be sold or traded for other required items not as easily obtained within the confines of their immediate environs. The males of a clan aged fifteen and over would be expected to fight for their chief should the need arise. The link between the chief, his people, and the land was incredibly strong, hence why the system endured into the eighteenth century.

After the Battle of Culloden in 1746, the London-based Government viewed the Highland way of life as a threat, and passed the Act of Proscription, bringing in laws to ensure the Clan system was broken up so that never again could it threaten the establishment and their authority. The long enduring link between chief, people, and land was brought to an abrupt end. Newly-appointed landowners did not see any monetary value in having people on the land, and began to look for more profitable ways to work their estates - primarily by the introduction of vast sheep farms.

The people were evicted to make way for these farms - evictions varied in their brutality. Some were allowed to resettle on the coastal fringes, and were given narrow strips of fairly poor land to do the best they could with. This became known as croft farming, and still exists today. Others went to the fast-growing urban centres like Glasgow, Dundee, Edinburgh, and the towns of the central lowlands to find work. But for many there was no other choice than to leave the land of their ancestors and to emigrate to the new world - America, Canada, Australia, New Zealand, South Africa, the Caribbean - in the hope of finding and carving out a new and better life than the one on offer in their own country. This period of mass emigration is called the 'Highland Clearances', and the legacy is still felt in Scotland - even to this day the Highlands is one of the most sparsely populated areas in Europe.

The remains of Clearance villages can be seen today throughout the Highlands, and serve as a reminder of this forced upheaval. The township at Arichonan is one of the haunting examples.

People once lived, loved, thrived and died on this land, and although they were not rich monetarily speaking, they had a strong sense of who they were and where they belonged. Their departure was forced upon them because of events beyond their control. We cannot rewrite history, but to visit places like Arichonan gives us an opportunity to reflect upon the actions taken by those who believed that sweeping entire communities from the land was 'progress'. The ancient Highland way of life was always going to be an awkward fit into a modern capitalist world - what would these communities be like today if they hadn't been evicted? Would they still exist? How would the people and their culture have adapted to fast changing times?

Perhaps we will never know the answers to these questions, but recent community land buyouts show the desire of the people to 'take back' what has been out with their control for so long. The Isle of Eigg, for example, was purchased by the local community on the twelfth of June 1997, and is now a thriving sustainable and self-sufficient island which is attracting more and more people.

Could the same happen at Arichonan, and many other places across Scotland? It is incredibly moving to walk around the ruins of the township and reflect upon this question. Arichonan is a truly special place, where people once lived, loved, thrived and died. It would be nice to think that one day people will return and thrive once more...

How to get there:

Arichonan Township is located in the west of Scotland, near the town of Lochgilphead on the A816. Turn off onto the B841 signposted for Cairnbaan. For a short distance you'll follow the line of the Crinan Canal, then turn left for Achnamara. Travel on this road for a short distance until you come to a War Memorial shaped like a Celtic cross, and veer to the right. When you see the Glean a Gealbhan car park (Forestry Commission) on the left, park and walk back up the track. Cross the road and follow the yellow way markers. You'll walk a short distance through what was a pine forest, and once you cross the wee burn you are nearly there.

77. Kilmartin and Kilmartin Glen

What you'll discover:

The whole of Kilmartin Glen is a venerable treasure trove of all things ancient and historic. It truly is a very special place with amazing and intriguing history literally around every corner. Although this book is mostly about seeking out singular special places, there is just so much in a relatively small area - three hundred and fifty ancient monuments within a six mile radius of the village of Kilmartin - that it is best to group everything together into one larger treasure.

Starting from the most ancient of times, at Achnabreck in the south of the glen, you'll find cup and spiral rock carvings. Nobody knows for sure what the rock art actually signifies, and the patterns themselves vary in style - what message were the people trying to convey, or was it just artistic expression? It is thought that the artwork goes back to around 4000 BCE which is the earliest that you tend to find these types of carvings in Scotland.

Moving a bit further forward in time to the Neolithic period from around 3000 BCE, and north of Achnabreck, you'll find a fascinating grouping of standing stones near Kilmartin village called Nether Largie. The stones have an eighteen and a half year lunar alignment, and also some intriguing cup marks carved on them, particularly the centrally located stone.

Very nearby at the Temple Wood there are two Neolithic stone circles with cairns inside, and one more simple circular cairn. From there you can walk the short distance down the road, and into the Bronze Age to visit a chambered burial cairn, dating from 2500 BCE.

You'd think that this would be more than enough history on display but no, a few miles south of Kilmartin you'll find Dunadd Hill Fort dating from around 500 CE (although I felt it was deserving of its own place in this book found at number 16).

In the cemetery of the Kirk Yard in Kilmartin village you can discover many Knight Templar gravestones. The Templar Knights fled persecution in the early fourteenth century after being branded as heretics by the Pope. They had very few countries in Europe to find any real safety, but Scotland was one of the few that did offer sanctuary. It is said by some historians that the Knight's journey took them by sea from France, around Ireland, and then onto Scotland from the west where they settled. When they died, these Knights received their distinctive Templar gravestones. There are many stories surrounding the Knights Templar in Scotland, and if you wish to know more I'd recommend 'The Temple and the Lodge', written by Michael Baigent and Richard Leigh. They certainly give some explanation as to why there is such a high density of Templar graves at Kilmartin, and other locations throughout Argyll if you're interested in looking.

After all the excitement and time travel, you'll need some refreshment, so pop into the Kilmartin museum and craft centre for some quality home-baked goods. For more history, visit the museum to see some of the artifacts that have been discovered locally over the years. Kilmartin Glen is a true gem of a place.

How to get there:

The sites mentioned above are found on or near the A816 between Kilmartin and Lochgilphead.

78. Skara Brae

What you'll discover:

The Orkney Isles are an archipelago of seventy islands located off the north coast of Scotland's mainland. They are no stranger to what I refer to as 'big weather', and when I first visited the islands in 2003, I was 'forced' to stay for a couple of extra days due to high winds. It was a blessing in disguise because it enabled me to take more time to enjoy the sights, sounds and history that lurks around every headland and bay of these amazing islands

As I drove north through Caithness on mainland Scotland to get the ferry to Stromness, I naively thought that Orkney would have the same low-lying moor-covered landscapes, but the reality couldn't have been further from my misguided preconceptions. Instead the Orkney Isles are a fertile, pastoral landscape, great for rearing livestock, and this is illustrated by the amount of small homestead buildings dotted all over the land, relying on agriculture and a sense of community.

This for me is one of the reasons that the ancient Neolithic settlement of Skara Brae is so interesting and intriguing, because it demonstrates a link with how people live today and how they lived over five thousand years ago. Skara Brae was first discovered in 1850 by a local farmer after a storm exposed two of the ancient houses. Due to being protected for millennia by sand dunes, when it was uncovered it gave us a window into the lives of our Neolithic ancestors. It serves as a time capsule, perfectly preserving the past.

The site dates back to around 3200 BCE, and consists of a village of eight houses or dwellings, built with dry stone walls and interlinking passageways. These passageways were built to provide protection from the aforementioned big weather, demonstrating the ingenuity of the people who built and lived in this community. Today access to see this amazingly well preserved site is by a path that overlooks the dwellings, where stone cupboards, hearths and bedding areas are clearly visible.

All of the artifacts that have been discovered are displayed in the visitor centre, including tools and jewellery. There is also a complete replica house which gives a great insight into the interior of the dwellings.

The final treasures of my book feature sites from the Orkney archipelago, some of which are part of the UNESCO World Heritage Sites 'Heart of Neolithic Orkney'. However there is so much more to discover on the Orkney Isles so my advice is to give yourself enough time to visit as much as possible.

How to get there:

Skara Brae is located on the western side of the mainland of Orkney near Sandwick, a short distance from the B9056. Skara Brae is in the care of Historic Environment Scotland, open all year round, and there is an admission fee to visit the site.

79. Tomb of the Eagles

What you'll discover:

The Isbister Chambered Cairn was first discovered in 1958 by a local farmer called Ronnie Simison, when he was digging along the edge of some flagstones. This Neolithic chambered cairn has been an absolute treasure trove of ancient artifacts, many of which are on display in the small family-run visitor centre (when you visit will find out that it can be a very hands on experience!).

Over time sixteen thousand human bones have been found, including over thirty human skulls. The human remains are fascinating because they allow historians, archaeologists and scientists to study diet as well as lifestyle and environment. What is also fascinating is that along with the human remains there were over seven hundred bones found, including many talons, from one main species of bird - the white-tailed sea eagle. Due to this discovery, the site is now more commonly known as the Tomb of the Eagles.

It has been discovered that these eagle remains date from around a thousand years after the cairn had been built. This proves that these cairns remained in use not only for a few but literally hundreds of generations, and that local custom with regards to the cairns and their ceremonial use changed over that length of time. Why the talons, why the sea eagle? When you visit, the excellent guides encourage you to think about these questions because there are a number of different theories.

The highlight for me was actually entering into the chambered cairn via a small tunnel, which is slightly claustrophobic. To think that this place has been here for so long, and used and revered by so many people is mind-boggling.

As you make your way to visit the Tomb of the Eagles, it is worth stopping at the Italian Chapel, a totally unique former Catholic Chapel that was built by Italian prisoners of war during World War Two. Once you have visited the Tomb, there are some great cliff-top walks nearby.

How to get there:

Located at the southernmost point of South Ronaldsay, travel to the end of the A961 and from there take the B9041. The Tomb is open seasonally and there is an admission fee to visit.

80. Ness and Ring of Brodgar

What you'll discover:

Since I was a child I have always loved history - the older the better as far as I was concerned. Until recently, it was believed that the concept of erecting ancient standing stones had come from Continental Europe, and had then travelled north to Stonehenge in England, and further north once again to Orkney. There was one major problem with this thesis - it was completely wrong.

It was always a quandary for many archaeologists and historians that the further north you travelled in the British Isles, the older the standing stone sites seemed to become. Thanks to recent discoveries on Orkney, history has been turned on its head and the books now have to be rewritten about standing stones and our understanding of them. The discovery of what can only really be described as a Neolithic temple site (the oldest in Europe) at the Ness of Brodgar has made historians re-evaluate everything that was previously understood about this part of our distant past.

Although the Ness of Brodgar is a more recent discovery, this area of Orkney is abundant with ancient historical sites. It is believed that the Ring of Brodgar, a stone circle to the west of the Ness, the Stones of Stenness to the east, the chambered cairn of Maeshowe, and other nearby sites, were all interconnected in some kind of spiritual way. It is absolutely amazing that from this rather unassuming location on a small archipelago of islands off the north coast of Scotland, ideas and a belief system evolved. The erecting of enormous megaliths started, developed, and then spread south, making the Ness of Brodgar and its associated monuments the centre of the Neolithic world in Western Europe. Stonehenge was therefore a much later model based upon what was found in the north.

Given that there were no metal tools or machinery available, these sites show that the ancient people of the north were incredibly resourceful in moving these huge stone slabs around and into place. Interestingly, it has been recently discovered that the technique involved the use of seaweed, in particular kelp which is abundant off the coast of much of the British Isles, and not rolling logs as previously thought.

What has also come to light is that the Ness of Brodgar, which was in use for over one thousand years, was deliberately decommissioned. It seems that this was done when the Neolithic (New Stone Age) was evolving into the Bronze Age. Rediscovered in 2003, excavations are ongoing and the site is only open to the public when these are in progress (usually beginning of July to the end of August).

Visiting the Ring of Brodgar and the Stones of Stenness are pretty straightforward, although to visit Maeshowe requires you to join a tour that departs from Skara Brae. Doing the tour is worthwhile because it will allow you to get inside the cairn, and as well as admiring the structure with its ancient history, you'll also be able to see Viking graffiti.

How to get there:

The whole area that covers these ancient sites is found a short distance from the main A965 road which connects the towns of Stromness and Kirkwall (Orkney's capital).

Epilogue

I have spent over fifteen years travelling around Scotland, in various sizes of vehicles with guests from all over the world. Each individual had their own expectations and desires of what Scotland was going to be like - these expectations could at times be hard to manage. With the mass of information and misinformation (or 'alternative facts' as they are now known) available about Scotland, it could be tough at times to let people down gently, and not be able to show them the Loch Ness Monster, Sir Sean Connery, or a wild haggis. However, with open hearts and minds, I managed to show thousands of visitors the 'real Scotland', and from my many adventures this book evolved.

The sheer number of people that I met over the years, along with the numerous and varied questions they asked, spurred me on to learn and research more about the country of my birth. Over the years whilst commentating on Scotland's history, landscapes and folklore, visitors would often say things like 'you should write a book'. Around Scotland in 80 Treasures was born because I wanted to continue to share my knowledge and love of Scotland.

To say that I feel lucky and privileged to have had the opportunity to travel to, visit, and experience the treasures written about in the book is an understatement. My desire to keep on searching for more treasure continues. I hope that you take the same amount of enjoyment and pleasure from the eighty treasures that Helen and I have, and we'd be delighted to hear of your experiences.

After all, what use is treasure if you don't share it with others?

Find us on Facebook: search 'Around Scotland in 80 Treasures'

Useful Information

Many of the sites in this guide are owned or looked after by organisations such as Historic Environment Scotland and the National Trust for Scotland so it is useful to have their contact information to help you on your travels.

Historic Environment Scotland | www.historicenvironment.scot | **0131 668 8600**
Treasures: 1, 3, 4, 5, 6, 8, 9, 12, 13, 15, 16, 17, 71, 77, 78 and 80

National Trust for Scotland | www.nts.org.uk | **0131 458 0200**
Treasures: 23, 70, 72 and 75

Walkhighlands is a very useful resource for detailed information on some the walks and places featured in this book.

Walkhighlands | www.walkhighlands.co.uk

The travel information below covers the ferry companies available for any boat trips, along with useful websites to check prior to setting off on your journey.

Traveline Scotland - journey planner | www.travelinescotland.com

Traffic Scotland - travel information | www.trafficscotland.org

Caledonian MacBrayne (Calmac) | www.calmac.co.uk
Treasures: 7, 29, 30, 31, 33, 34, 35, 36, 39, 47, 50, 51, 52 and 59

Northlink / Pentland Ferries | www.northlinkferries.co.uk / www.pentlandferries.co.uk
Treasures: 78, 79 and 80 (Orkney Isles)

Staffa Trips / Turus Mara | www.staffatrips.co.uk / www.turusmara.com
Treasures: 7 and 32 (Iona and Staffa)

Bella Jane / Misty Isle | www.bellajane.co.uk / www.mistyisleboattrips.co.uk
Treasure: 38

Glenelg Ferry | www.skyeferry.co.uk
Treasure: 41

The following information covers the independently owned treasures:

Fatlips Castle | www.fatlipscastle.com
Treasure: 11

Dunnottar Castle | www.dunnottarcastle.co.uk
Treasure: 19

Wormistoune House and Gardens |
www.discoverscottishgardens.org/garden/wormistoune-house
Treasure: 22

Lochinver Larder | www.piesbypost.co.uk
Treasure: 42

Cromars Fish and Chip Shop | www.cromars.co.uk
Treasure: 44

Loch Fyne Oyster Bar / Fyne Ales | www.lochfyne.com / www.fyneales.com
Treasure: 46

Abhainn Dearg Distillery | www.abhainndearg.co.uk
Treasure: 47

The Govan Stones | www.thegovanstones.org.uk
Treasure: 64

The Great Polish Map of Scotland | www.mapascotland.org
Treasure: 65

The Kelpies | www.thehelix.co.uk
Treasure: 66

Gilmerton Cove | www.gilmertoncove.org.uk
Treasure: 69

Author Acknowledgements

Helen and I's friend Kate inspired the title of this book in an off the cuff comment after we'd all had a few gins, so thank you to Kate for giving me the idea of Around Scotland in 80 Treasures.

In January 2002 my sister-in-law Irene spotted a tiny job advertisement in a newspaper looking for 'young, Scottish and enthusiastic' people to become tour guides. After a bit of encouragement from her I applied and got the job – and the content of Around Scotland in 80 Treasures has come largely from the fifteen years I spent as a tour guide. So I must thank Irene for her sharp eyesight!

Through my time in tourism I met and made many wonderful friends, had some truly amazing experiences, and even reunited with an old school friend from as far back as my playgroup days aged three; but most importantly of all I met and married my life partner Helen, without whom I would not be the person I am today. Without Helen's support, help, patience and hard work this book would never have happened, so a very special thank you to her for everything – words are not enough to convey my love and gratitude.

The journey through Scottish tourism also allowed me to make other important contacts like Neil Hamilton, who expertly designed the cover and treasure maps featured throughout this book; his patience and design abilities are so greatly appreciated. I must also thank Karen Marr and Neil McLennan, two tour guiding friends, for the use of their fine photography.

Picture Credits

All images © Helen Keith with the following exceptions:

© David Keith – Treasures: 2 (1st photo), 3, 10, 11, 12, 22, 45 (4th photo), 49 (2nd photo), 64, 66 (2nd photo), 67, 71, 74, 76 and thistle photo in introduction

© Karen Marr Photography (www.kmarrphotography.com) – Treasures: 4 (3rd photo), 7 (1st photo), 8, 25 (2nd photo), 27 (2nd photo), 28, 33 (1st photo), 34 (2nd photo), 36 (2nd photo), 37 (2nd photo), 38 (1st photo), 43 (2nd photo), 60 (1st photo), 62 (1st photo), 63, 66 (1st photo), 70, 75, 77, 78 (2nd photo), 80 (4th photo) and harebell photo in introduction

© Neil McLennan – Treasures: 58, 72, 73, 78 (1st photo), 79, 80 (1st, 2nd & 3rd photos)

© Susannah Skiver Barton – Treasure 2 (2nd & 3rd photos)

© Graham Keith – Treasure 25 (1st photo)

© Alan Rowan (@MunroMoonwalker) – Treasure 41: Glenelg sign

© Craig Allardyce (@csa_adventure) – Treasure 65: Great Polish Map of Scotland

iStock.com/theasis – Treasure 5: Inchmahome Priory
iStock.com/SaraEdwards – Treasure 18: Castle Moil
iStock.com/Gannet77 – Treasure 45: Arbroath Smokies

Treasure 59: The Ringing Stone – cc-by-sa/2.0 - © Andrew Curtis – geography.org.uk/p/5466830

Cover and maps by Neil Hamilton

All information correct at the time of writing; the author takes no responsibility for any inaccuracies that are beyond the author's control.

Printed in Great Britain
by Amazon